Filipinos Are Austronesians

By
Emmanuel Ikan Astillero
and Friends

Preface

This modest book came to be written because of Facebook exchanges between Filipino friends: Tiz Wezza of Australia, Joey Miguel of New Zealand, and myself.

Our conversations in FB revealed that we are not just "Filipinos", a name given to us by Spanish colonizers in 1564, when Miguel Lopez de Legazpi occupied Maynila and declared the whole territory, as "owned" by the Spanish monarch (Phillip or Felipe), and all peoples within it, as subjects of the Spanish crown.

Tiz and Joey sent me a lot of materials since October 2017 which I kept and now use them for a sketch history of us Filipinos – as part of a larger Austronesian family of peoples in the Pacific.

We share customs, traditions, culture, artifacts, textile weave designs, houses of nipa, family-closeness, remembrance of ancestors, food types, traits, language, food, herbs, boat-designs, our brown skin and our physiognomy – with our cousins spread over 54 billion square miles of the Pacific Ocean and its adjacent seas and islands.

Our cousins are in the farthest west in Madagascar, adjacent to the "black continent" of Africa, easternmost to "Rapa Nui" or the Easter Islands where a remnant of Polynesians remain under the governance of Chile, a South American government.

We are cousins to the Hawaiians to the north of the Pacific who, themselves, came from Tahiti, in the middle of the Pacific, and southernmost to New Zealand – the Maoris.

Our closest relatives are in the ASEAN (Association of SouthEast Asian Nations).

There are four parts: An Overview, Part One about Austronesians in general, Part Two are sketches of particular countries, Part Three is a pictorial of "Old Philippines, capped by a "fast-forward" to 2015, when a beautiful Filipina Austronesian with European blood, won the title of Miss Universe; and Part Four, The Philippines Today.

Emmanuel ikan Astillero
1592 Camino de la Fe, Guadalupe Nuevo, Makati City, 1212 PHILIPPINES
e-mail astilleroe@gmail.com, noelastillero@yahoo.com
Facebook: "Emmanuel Ikan Astillero"

October 6, 2017 (my 78th birthday)

Ooooo

Introduction

The idea of doing a book – completely from online sources – came to me as I was exchanging conversations in FB with two friends: Tiz Wezza who is a Filipino in Australia, and Joey Miguel, a Filipino in New Zealand. Together, these two were sending me materials about Austronesians in Australia and in New Zealand. Tiz sent me alsop materials from Indonesia and Malaysia.

Where I can cite the sources of texts and pictures, I do – putting the URL, and other Internet sources.

It is a voyage of rediscovery – of my roots. I didn't know, until now, that Filipinos are of Austronesian stock, originally from Taiwan, and perhaps, from Japan.

From the Northern Philippines, our Indigenous tribes bear witness that we are close cousins of Polynesians, Micronesians, Melanesians. From the Philippines, the Austronesians stayed in Northern Luzon, then sailed to the wide Pacific Ocean – to as far north inHawaii and south to New Zealand, east to Easter Island (Rapa Nui), and west to Madagascar.

Our kinship is borne by language, DNA-genes, brown skin, almost one facial structure and physiognomy, customs and traditions, traditional clothes – weave, color, design; animist religion before Islam and Christianity, and boat-building.

There is a trove of history, of about 3,000 years old, of our people.

Emmanuel I. Astillero

ooooo

Very Important Notice to the Readers

While this book will be sold, it is not a commercial undertaking because all, repeat, all, the proceeds, minus costs incurred in publishing/printing and distribution/shipping, shall go into a trust fund for the creation of a "Philippine Austronesian Institute", based in Metro Manila, Philippines, and with affiliates or branches in Austronesian societies in the Pacific and in Southeast Asia.

The purpose, and goal, of this organization is to keep alive the indigenous spiritual beliefs, customs, tradition, music, art, dances, weavig designs, dresses, architecture, literature, publications, scientific research on Austronesian archaeology, anthropology, and related sciences – as well as all spiritual and physical aspects of our large Austronesian Family. This is especially true in the Philippines where the concept of an "Austronesian" is all but obliterated by foreign colonialism, mass consumerism and mass media.

The Trust Fund, among others, will contribute to a periodic gathering of Austronesian musician, dancers, painters, and other public performers in Metro Manila, as well as elsewhere in the major cities of the Austronesian world. It will support the "Festival Pasipika" that has been held successfully in New Zealand and Guahan (Guam). We plan to establish an Austronesian Museum with replicas of Austronesian artifacts gathered from all over.

By this same Notice, the copyright of this book is provided free for public use, for non-profit uses - in the same spirit that the editor used social media, online at "free public use", for the pictures, texts, and other materials used in this book.

Thank you.

Emmanuel Ikan Astillero - astilleroe@gmail.com

January 10, 2017

Austronesia-13/01/2018

Table of Contents

Preface ………………………………………………………… Page 1
Introduction …………………………………………………… Page 2
Very Important Notice ………………………………………… Page 3

Overview ……………………………………………………… Page 6
    Pasipika Festival ………………………………… Page 7
    Name Change …………………………………… Page 7
    Religion Change ………………………………… Page 8

Part One. The Widespread Austronesian Family ………... Page 10
    Austronesian Language Speakers …………………… Page 10
    Migration Flow from Taiwan to the Pacific ………… Page 12
    Filipino Balangay Boat ………………………………… Page 13
    Austronesian Lineage Graphics ……………………… Page 14
    ASEAN ………………………………………………… Page 15
    Polynesia ……………………………………………… Page 18
    Melanesia ……………………………………………… Page 22
        The Sweet Potato ……………………………… Page 29
        Malays: the Philippines, Indonesia, Malaysia . Page 30
        Austronesian Numerals/Similarity of "Dog"….. Page 31-32
        Phonetic Comparison between Filipino-Cebuano,
        Borneo-Kadazan, and Bahasa Melayu ……… Page 32-33
    Micronesia ……………………………………………… Page 34

Part Two. Sketches of Major Austronesian Locations….. Page 35
    Brunei Darusalaam …………………………………… Page 37
    Cambodia – Cham People …………………………… Page 39
    Chile – Rapa Nui – Easter Island …………………… Page 44
    China-Taiwan-Formosa ……………………………… Page 47
    Cook Islands …………………………………………… Page 51
    East Timor – Timor Leste …………………………… Page 54
    Fiji ……………………………………………………… Page 57
    French Polynesia ……………………………………… Page 60
    Guam & Northern Marianas …………………………… Page 62
    Hawaii (U.S.A.)………………………………………… Page 70
    Indonesia ……………………………………………… Page 77
    Kiribati ………………………………………………… Page 80
    Madagascar …………………………………………… Page 84
        "Madagascar Beauties"………………………… Page 88
    Malaysia ……………………………………………… Page 90
        "Austronesian Sea Dwellers"-Orang Laut…… Page 94-95
    Marshall Islands ……………………………………… Page 96

"Rising Seas Claiming Nation"	Page 100
Micronesia	Page 106
"Sailing the Pacific"	Page 107
Nauru	Page 109
New Caledonia	Page 112
New Zealand (Maori)	Page 118
Palau	Page 124
Papua New Guinea (Outer Islands)	Page 128
Philippines	Page 134
"Young Woman Rules Mandaya Land"	Page 139
Samoa	Page 143
Solomon Islands	Page 146
Thailand	Page 149
Tonga	Page 153
"Tonga Once Heart of Mighty Empire"	Page 153
Tuvalu	Page 155
Vanuatu	Page 158
Viet Nam	Page 160
Part Three. Old Philippines	Page 162
Part Four. The Philippines Today (upto - 2018)	Page 194
Pia Alonso Wurtzbach	Page 194
President Digong	Page 195
Secrets of Underdevelopment	Page 196

Filipinos are Austronesians

By Emmanuel Ikan Astillero, Bailen, Cavite, Philippines[1]

Overview

"Austronesian" comes from the Greek for 'south' and 'island.' Or "people of the southern islands". Originating from the aborigines of Japan and Taiwan, they spread southwards, via the Philippines, to the wide Pacific, occupying islands since about 3,000 years BCE (Before Common Era).

The Austronesians are "boat people" – intrepid sea-farers. Sailing the uncharted waters, they are the "brown" people found from Madagascar to Easter Island, and migrated from Taiwan and Southern Japan about 3,000 years ago to Northern Philippines. They stayed in the Philippines, mostly in Northern Luzon, for a millennium, before sailing forth to the Pacific Ocean islands, as far north as Hawai'i and as far south to New Zealand.

An Austronesian seafarer. (Photo credit; Joey Miguel, FB, Oct. 2017)

Filipinos comprise over a fourth of the estimated (2015) 400 million Austronesians scattered from Taiwan to the Philippnes, to Hawaii in North Pacific to New Zealand in the south, and Easter Islands in Chile. Almost 1,300 languages are spoken, averaging 300,000 people per language.

Most Filipinos do not know their Austronesian core identity, having settled down and became farmers and townspeople – not anymore seafarers hopping from island-to-island. That was at least a thousand years ago.

---

[1] *Emmanuel Ikan Astillero is a licensed Environmental Planner (PRC-0000040), and a member of the Philippine Institute of Environmental Planners (PIEP), based in the School of Urban-Regional Planning, University of the Philippines, Diliman Campus, Quezon City Philippines.*

The more than 300 years rule of Spain and the forced imposition of the Catholic Church upon the helpless natives submerged the Austronesian consciousness in the Philippines.

Pasipika Festival.
Filipinos have genetic, linguistic and cultural links with Micronesia, Melanesia, and Polynesia. These linkages have been scientifically established by anthropologists, archeologists, and etymologists. There are "Festivals Pasipika", the last one in 2016 held in Guam, and cultural dancers and singers from as far as Rapa Nui, east of the Pacific, in South America, came.[2] A similar Pasipika Festival was held in New Zealand the previous year.

Has the Philippines sent delegations of singers and dancers to these festivals? We see no record of their participation – either online or in You Tube.

"The Austronesians are the Filipinos (mostly Austronesian), the Indonesians (20% Austronesian), the coastal New Guineans (25% Austronesian), the Polynesians (50% Austronesian) and the Micronesians (35% Austronesian). Also Malays appear to have some unknown Austronesian element. There is also some Austronesian in the Vietnamese and the Khmer. All of these are in whole or in part Austronesians."[3]

However, successive cultural layers of foreign invasions and influences have turned Filipino Austronesians into westernized Asians. The advent of Christianity in 1521, and the subsequent colonization of the Philippines, in 1564, contributed to the westernization of the Filipinos. The Americans, emphasizing public education and public health, completed this westernizing cultural inroads into the Filipino psyche.

While Spain did not teach Filipinos Spanish, the Americans taught them English. The native Austronesian languages, numbering over 100, survived – e.g., Ilocano, Pampango, Tagalog, Bicolano, Waray, Ilonggo, Cebuhano or "Bisaya", and the languages of the Moro tribes in Mindanao, e.g., Maranao, Tausog, Maguindanao, etc..

Name Change.
Today, most Filipinos have shed their native names and dresses, use Spanish and American names, and sport western-style clothes. Names like "Luningning", "Liwayway", "Lapu-Lapu", have been replaced by "Pedro", "Juan", "William", "Maria".

Having mastered the English language, Filipinos have spread globally as "OFWs" ("Overseas Foreign Workers") in search of jobs. Their families remain behind. On the positive side, the OFWs remit their earnings back to the Philippines. Their remittance is the biggest source of foreign exchange earnings, running into billions of US dollars.

Some Filipinos still share cultural customs, clothes and traditions similar with their Austronesian cousins in the Pacific islands. But these are mostly "indigenous peoples" ("IPs") or the tribes occupying the mountainous regions of the Philippines. The Austronesian tradition show up in

---

[2] *Check "You Tube" – Austronesian People.*
[3] *"Beyond Highbrow" – Robert Lindsay, Blog, Internet – Free Public Use <June 9 2009>*

dances and music of the IPs – in the Mountain Provinces of Luzon (e.g., the Aetas/Agtas, Bugkalot, Ifugao, Ibaloi, Kalinga, Apayao, etc.) and in Mindanao (e.g., Manobo, Mandaya, T'boli, B'laan, Maranao, etc.).

Religion Change. The lowland Filipinos have become westernized. The religions of 95% of Filipinos are borrowed from the Middle East: 85% profess Christianity, 10% Islam, and the rest are pre-colonial native beliefs of "indigenous peoples". But underneath the patina of Christianity or Islam are ceremonies and incantations to the nature spirits of the mountains, the rivers, stones, trees, the sky, etc. Filipinos, despite Christianity and islam, still believe in the unseen spirits of dead ancestors and of the dark forests. On occasions of thanksgiving, they offer food to these spirits.

The traditional shamans and priestesses of the Austronesian migrants might have been replaced by Catholic and Protestant priests and pastors, and Islamic imams in their island destinations, but old traits, customs, tradition, and physical characteristics remain to relate the progenies of these adventurous people true to their indigenous Austronesian culture. The Spanish friars might have burned the "anito's" of the natives, but belief in these nature spirits live on – physically in the statuettes in the Mountain Province, but mainly, in the psyche of even lowland Christians, who still offer food to these spirits to propitiate bad omens.

Bulul fertility idols guard the Banaue rice terraces in Mt. Province, Luzon, Phils. **(Photo credit: Pinterest)**

Banaue Rice Terraces, Mt. Province, North Luzon – providing similar cultural Austronesian heritage also seen in Indonesia, Malaysia, and as far west as Madagascar. (Photo credit: Pinterest)

All over the Pacific islands and Southeast Asia are the ubiquitous "nipa huts" or the Filipino "bahay kubo". The "buko" (young green coconut) is a universal drink all over the Pacific and Island Southeast Asia because the coconut tree, the "tree of life" – from whence many household and food items can be had - is always there.

There is a Pacific-wide awareness of Austronesia. Cultural festivals, held, for instance, in New Zealand ("Pasipika Festival", 2015), saw participants come from far-flung Austronesian groups. These periodic gathering of kinsmen clearly showcase the living culture of the Austronesians in the Pacific islands. Maoris from New Zealand have visited Taiwan to trace their Austronesian lineage. They found them in the aborigine tribe of the Yamis in Taiwan.

Part One. The Widespread Austronesian Family

(Text and map, below, from Tiz Wezza, FB, Oct 2017).

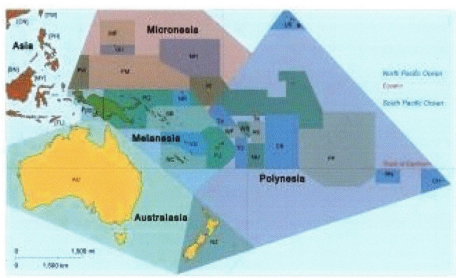

Austronesian-speaking people may be found in various distinct ethnic groups in Southeast Asia, Oceania and East Africa. Their language have been traced, etymologically, to the Austronesian family of languages. They originated from Taiwanese aborigines (principally, the Yamis). From Taiwan they spread southwards to the Philippines, Malaysia, East Timor, Indonesia, Brunei, Cocos (Keeling) Islands, Madagascar, Micronesia, and Polynesia. The Malay people of Singapore, the Polynesian peoples of New Zealand and Hawaii, and the non-Papuan people of Melanesia belong to this family. Austronesian speakers are in the regions of the Pattani in Thailand, the Cham areas in Vietnam and Cambodia, and the Hainan region of China, parts of Sri Lanka, southern Myanmar, southern tip of South Africa, Suriname and some of the Andaman Islands. The people of the Maldives also possess traces of Austronesian genes via gene flow from the Malay Archipelago. The territories populated by Austronesian-speaking peoples are known collectively as Austronesia. *(Data source: Wikipedia)*

Austronesian Language Speakers

amount to 400 million. The countries are:

- Indonesia: 260,581,000 (2016)
- Philippines: est. 104,494,000
- Madagascar: over 20,000,000 (2011)
- Malaysia: 14,290,000 (2010) - Malays
- United States: 4,816,144 (migrants)
- Papua New Guinea: 1,300,000 (Melanesians, excluding Papuans)

- East Timor: 1,167,242 (2015)
- New Zealand: 855,000 (2006) - Maoris
- Brunei: 724,000? (2006)
- Singapore: over 700,000 (Malay only)
- Solomon Islands: 478,000 (2005)
- Taiwan: 480,000 (2006)
- Fiji: 456,000 (2005)
- Australia: 210,843
- Samoa: 193,773 (2015)
- Tonga: 105,323
- Northern Mariana Islands: 52,344
- Hawaii: 140,652 or 401,162
- Suriname: 71,000 (2009)
- Sri Lanka 40,189 (2012)
- Chile: 5,682 (Rapa Nui or Easter Islands)

In an interview, the noted archeologist, Peter Bellwood, said that "...the early Austronesians ...[and]...their Pre-Austronesian ancestors moved as Neolithic and probably rice- and millet-cultivating populations from Fujian to Taiwan between 5,000 and 6,000 years ago. In Taiwan, they developed what linguists reconstruct today as 'Proto-Austronesian' (no Austronesian speakers ever inhabited southern China according to linguistic records, but Pre-Austronesian ones obviously did), and honed their coastal economies for more than a millennium before moving on into the Batanes Islands and the northern Philippines at about 4,000 years ago, carrying with them traditions of making red-slipped pottery, ornaments of Taiwan (Fengtian) jade, polished and sometimes stepped stone adzes, domesticated crops, pigs and dogs, and of course a well-developed maritime tradition of fishing and canoe construction, using sails. The prehistory of the Austronesian world is far too complex to summarise here, but it is important to remember that it took more than 3,000 years for colonists to spread gradually, from island to island, until they finally reached New Zealand around AD 1250, via the islands of central and eastern Polynesia." [4]

"The Austronesian-speaking peoples are various populations in Oceania and Southeast Asia that speak languages of the Austronesian family. They include Taiwanese aborigines; the majority ethnic groups of East Timor, Indonesia, Malaysia, the Philippines, Brunei, Madagascar, Micronesia, and Polynesia, as well as the Polynesian peoples of New Zealand and Hawaii, and the non-Papuan people of Melanesia. They are also found in Singapore, the Pattani region of Thailand, and the Cham areas of Vietnam (remnants of the Champa kingdom which covered

---

[4] Hsiao-chun Hung "New Perspectives in Southeast Asian and Pacific Prehistory", Australian National University, Press Library. (Published online for free public use.)

central and southern Vietnam), Cambodia, and Hainan, China. The territories populated by Austronesian-speaking peoples are known collectively as Austronesia."[5]

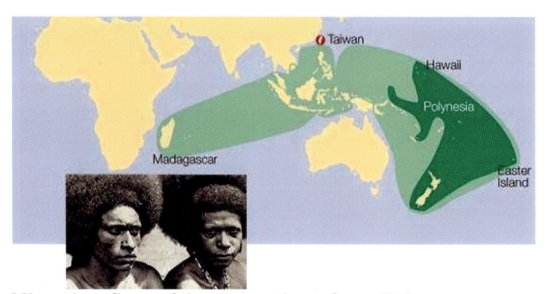

Migration flow of Austronesians from Taiwan. (From "New research into the origins of the Austronesian languages", January 28, 2016, University of Huddersfield; Read more at: https://phys.org/news/2016-01-austronesian-languages.html#jCp)

 Austronesian Yamis – aborigines of Taiwan. (Wiki – the Free Encyclopedia)

---

[5] *<Forumbiodiversity.com>. Check out these URLs:* http://www.youtube.com/embed/mYSr2k4buqU; http://en.wikipedia.org/wiki/Austronesian_peoples; http://www.youtube.com/watch?v=oShir...cdRVAAAAAAAAA

Filipino Balangay Boat. In the Philippines, an Austronesian boat found preserved in the swamps of Butuan City, in Surigao, Philippines, is called "balangay" from which the modern Pilipino term for "community" or village is derived: "barangay". It is said that the "balangay's" carried complete communities into the Philippines.

The picture below shows a "Balangay" anchored in Manila Bay. A Filipina woman climber of Mt. Everest, will sail in 2018 with a team to Guangzhou in China to retrace Chinese trade routes to the Philippines.

A replica of the original "balangay" boat of Butuan City moored at Manila Bay, with the skyscrapers of Roxas Boulevard, Pasay, Metro Manila in the background. (Photo credit and data source: Dra. Cora Pe-Benito Claudio, FB sent to the author, Nov 2017.)

Austronesian Lineage Graphics, below, (Photo credit: Facebook - Downloaded from the Internet, Free Public Onine Use)

Austronesian-People:

Native-Taiwanese
Jomon-people(native-japanese)+Ainu
Borneo-tribes
Luzon-groups
Chamic-tribes
Igorot-tribes
Lumad-tribes
Malagasy-tribes
Melanesian-tribes
Micronesian-tribes
Moken-groups
Moro-tribes
Polynesian-tribes
Indonesian-tribes
Visayan-tribes

Decedants of Austronesians:

Taiwanese people;
Japanese people;
south-east-coast-"chinese" Min;
Madagascar-tribes;
some south-american tribes on west-coast;
...

Total-Population: ~550.000.000 people

Genetically, Cultural and linguistic connection

Austronesian languages are spoken in Brunei, Cambodia, Chile, China, Cook Islands, East Timor, Fiji, French Polynesia, Guam, Indonesia, Kiribati, Madagascar, Malaysia, Marshall Islands, Mayotte, Micronesia, Myanmar, Nauru, New Caledonia, New Zealand, Niue, Northern Mariana Islands, Palau, Papua New Guinea, Philippines, Samoa, Solomon Islands, Suriname, Taiwan, Thailand, Tokelau, Tonga, Tuvalu, USA, Vanuatu, Viet Nam, Wallis and Futuna. The total number of speakers of Austronesian languages is estimated at 311,740,132.

ASEAN. The present ASEAN (Association of SouthEast Asian Nations) is a gathering of part of this large family. The nation-members of ASEAN are blood cousins. (A map of Southeast Asia is below.)

Photo: asean.org, online.

The Association of Southeast Asian Nations is a regional intergovernmental organisation comprising ten Southeast Asian states which promotes Pan-Asianism and intergovernmental cooperation and facilitates (Wikipedia)

Founded: 8 August 1967. Headquarters: Jakarta, Indonesia. Members: Thailand, Vietnam, Indonesia, Malaysia, Philippines, Singapore, Myanmar (Burma), Cambodia, Laos, Brunei.

The chair for 2016 was the Philippines, led by President Rodrigo Roa Duterte.

- ASEAN's combined GDP tops $2.6 trillion: 3rd largest in Asia, 7th in the world.
- With over 600 million people, the ASEAN market is larger than the EU or North America.

The ASEAN countries. (Map credit: Omni Online Marketing.)

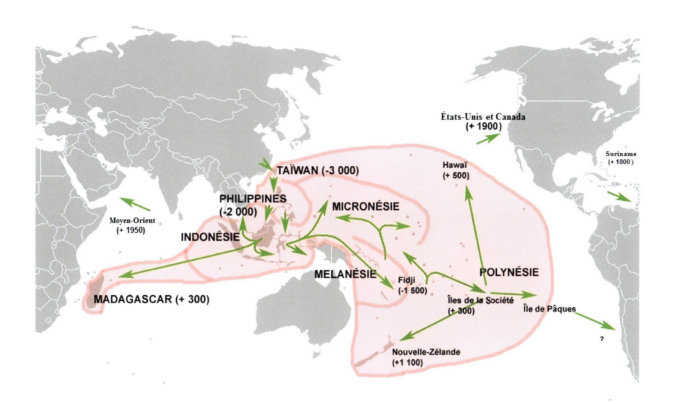

Map showing the migration of Austronesians from Taiwan and southwards to the Pacific. *(Map Source: FB, Tiz Wezza, op.cit).*

There are three major cultural areas in the Pacific Ocean: Melanesia, Micronesia, and Polynesia.

Out of Taiwan, and perhaps, farther north, from the Ainus of Japan, the Austronesians spread to areas of the Pacific: Southeast Asia, Micronesia, Melanesia, and Polynesia, and the outer islands of Australia and New Zealand.

Polynesia is a major part of Austronesia. The map below locates the Polynesians. The more popular tourist destination islands are Hawaii and Tahiti. The American battles vs Japan in World War (1942-1945) are chronicled in these Pacific islands, e.g., Guadalcanal, Iwo Jima, Coral Sea, Midway, Leyte Gulf, etc.

Polynesia

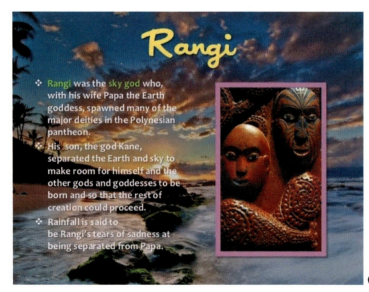 Gods and Goddesses of Polynesia.

(Photo Credit: Tiz Wezza, FB, Nov 2017)

"Polynesia" is from Greek word "many islands". It is a group of over a thousand islands spread over the Pacific Ocean. First used by Charles de Brosses in 1756 to all the islands of the Pacific, they are those islands within a triangle defined north at the Hawaiian Islands, south at

New Zealand, and east at Easter Island. Polynesian Tuvalu is an island group outside this triangle; there are smaller Polynesian groups in the Solomon Islands and in Vanuatu.

(Map source: FB Free Public Use, online.)

Below. Polynesian Hula dancers. (Photo credit – downloaded from the Internet, Free Public Use)

Below. Tahitian male dancers. (Pic credit – downloaded from the Internet)

(Below) Tahitian female dancers- showing the affinity of grass skirts with other Austronesian dancers in Melanesia and Hawaii. (Photo credit – downloaded from the Internet, Free Public Online Use)

Polynesia is in Oceania, which comprises more than 1,000 islands in the central and southern Pacific Ocean. The indigenous people of Polynesia, like many other Pacific Islanders, are descendants of Austronesian-speaking navigators who first settled western Polynesia as long ago as 3,000 years.

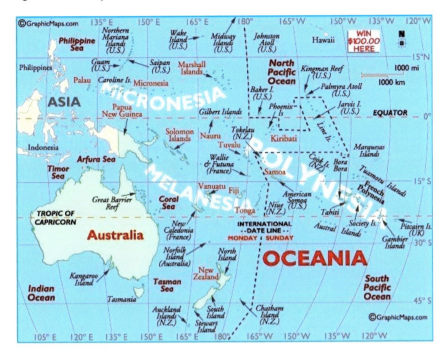

Map credit: Tiz Wezza, FB page cover- <Pacific Culture for Filipino Agnostics and Atheists>

"Polynesia" was coined in 1756 by Charles de Brosses, a French writer, who applied it to all the islands of the Pacific. It was limited, however, to islands in the Polynesian Triangle: from Hawai`i, to New Zealand (Aotearoa) and to Easter Island (Rapa Nui). Within this Triangle are Samoa, Tonga, the Cook Islands, Tuvalu, Tokelau, Niue, Wallis and Futuna, and French Polynesia.

Polynesian settlements in Melanesia: Papua New Guinea, the Solomon Islands and Vanuatu, include the Caroline Islands in Micronesia. Rotuma, north of Fiji is an island group with Polynesian culture outside the Polynesian Triangle. Tonga, within the triangle, is linked culturally and historically with some of the Lau Islands, southeast of Fiji.

Most of the Pacific Austronesian groups are in New Zealand and Hawaii: of about 118,000 sq mi (300,000 or 310,000 sq km) of land, more than 103,000 sq mi (270,000 sq km) are in New Zealand; the Hawaiian archipelago comprises half the remainder. Geologically, the oldest rocks are in New Zealand - about 510 million years old, while. the oldest Polynesian rocks are in the Hawaiian Emperor Seamount Chain – about 80 million years old.

The Polynesian people are sea-migrating Austronesian people. The Polynesian languages originated in the Malay Archipelago, finally traced back to Taiwan, from where, via the Philippines, about 3000 and 1000 BCE, Austronesians languages spread from Taiwan into Island Southeast Asia (ISEA).

Melanesia

(Above) The geographical extent of Melanesia. (Map source: Internet public online free to download).

Melanesia is a subregion of Oceania extending from New Guinea island in the southwestern Pacific Ocean to the Arafura Sea, and eastward to Fiji. The region includes the four countries of Vanuatu, the Solomon Islands, Fiji, and Papua New Guinea.

Besides these independent countries, Melanesia also includes: New Caledonia, a special collectivity of France; and Western New Guinea Region of Indonesia, within Papua Province and West Papua Province on western New Guinea island and adjacent small islands.

The name *Melanesia* (in French *Mélanésie* from the Greek μέλας, *black*, and νῆσος, *islands*) was first used by Jules Dumont d'Urville in 1832 to denote an ethnic and geographical grouping of islands whose inhabitants he thought were distinct from those of Micronesia and Polynesia.

The Pasifika Festival in New Zealand is very popular annual festival and attracts participants from Austronesian groups.

The map below locates Melanesia, whose major groups are in Papua New Guinea and its outer islands, extending up to near New Zealand.

Melanesia, a subregion of Oceania, extends from New Guinea island in the southwestern Pacific Ocean to the Arafura Sea, and eastward to Fiji.

The area covers Vanuatu, the Solomon Islands, Fiji, and Papua New Guinea. It also includes New Caledonia, and Western New Guinea of Indonesia, within Papua Province and West Papua Province on western New Guinea island and adjacent small islands.

Jules Dumont d'Urville in 1832 first used *"Melanesia "* - from the Greek "black islands" because of the dark complexion of the inhabitants, as they were distinct from those of Micronesia and Polynesia.

The Pasifika Festival is very popular in New Zealand. New Zealand has large numbers of Maori, Samoans, Tongans, Cook Islanders and other Polynesian groups.

A popular Melanesian festival, "Hiri Moale", see below, is celebrated annually where a boat is decked out and dancers display their talents. The boat is said to be loaded with pots and other ceramic items, and taken to the mainland of Papua New Guinea, to be used for storing "sago" – the starch extract from trees in the islands. The boat returns to the Outer Islands after a year, laden with fruits and food.

Sago being extracted from a fallen palm tree. (Photo credit: downloaded from the Internet, Free Public Online Use, c/o Joey Miguel, NZ/FB)

Hiri Moale.

Hiri Moale, above, celebrated annually in Melanesian part of Papua New Guinea, remembering the exchange of pots to the outer islands for sago. (Photo credit: downloaded from the Internet, Joey Miguel, FB)

A Melanesian dancer during the Hiri Moale festival in Papua New Guinea. Note the boat she is carrying on her left hand. It is similar to the Filipino "balangay boat" (see p.6 – Overview, above). (Photo credit: downloaded from the Internet, Joey Miguel, FB)

Melanesians of Papua New Guinea, Pasipika Festival, 2015. (Photo credit: downloaded from the Internet, Joey Miguel, FB)

Melanesians. Austronesians mixed with older African lineage in Papua New Guinea (PNG).The Africans arrived in PNG 50-40,000 BCE, predating the arrival of Austronesians who came in the "outer islands" of PNG 3,000 years BCE. (Photo credit: downloaded from the Internet, c/´ Joey Miguel, FB, Free Public Use Online)

Modern mix of Melanesians with Indian and Asian heritage. This is the "Pasipika Festival" in New Zealand, 2015. (Photo credit: downloaded from the Internet, Joey Miguel, FB)

Left. A Melanesian dancer performing during the Pasipika Festival, 2015 at New Zealand. (Photo credit: downloaded from the Internet, Joey Miguel, FB, Free Public Use Online)

"DNA shows how the sweet potato crossed the seas"

Photo credit: Topic Photo Agency/Corbis

Austronesians ate sweet potatoes as a staple root crop of for the last 1,000 years. It is a native of South America; an immigrant to the Pacific. It spread throughout Polynesia and the surrounding Pacific islands. Modern crops indicate that Austronesians visited South America before the Europeans came in the 15th century.

Polynesia calls the sweet potato (*Ipomoea batatas*) 'kuumala', 'kumara', 'cumar' or 'cumal' among Quechua speakers in northwestern South America; "camote" in the Philippines. The names indicate that the tuber proliferated in Polynesia after an early introduction by locals who visited South America, before Europeans came (1492 and onwards. Or the natural dispersal of seeds across the Pacific Ocean reached Oceania.

Archaeologist Douglas Yen, then at the Museum in Honolulu, Hawaii, noted a 'tripartite' hypothesis, published recently in the *Proceedings of the National Academy of Sciences,* in the 1970s, which says that the sweet potato arrived in Oceania - first, between 1000 and 1100 BCE after Polynesian voyagers visited South America. It then spread it to other Pacific islands.

The Spaniards arrived in the Philippines March 1521 and established a formal colonial government in 1564 with a capital in Manila. large farms, called *encomiendas* (now called "hacienda's) covering thousands of hectares, were awarded to loyal Spanish soldiers and religious orders. These farms introduced export crops, such as tobacco and coffee, for onward trade to Spain via Mexico - the *Galleon Trade*. Sweet-potato were also planted in these encomiendas in the Philippines and in the Spanish possessions in the western Pacific, such as Guahan (Guam).

(Data source from Brian Switek (21 January 2013), citing Roullier, C., Benoit, L., McKey, D. B. & Lebot, V. Proc. Natl Acad. Sci. USA http://dx.doi.org/10.1073/pnas.1211049110 (2013); Yen, D. E. The Sweet Potato in Oceania: An Essay in Ethnobotany (Bishop Mus. Press, 1974).

Malays: the Philippines, Indonesia and Malaysia

People of these three countries are popularly named "Malays", or "Melayu". In Pilipino, "Melayu" or "malayo" means "far" indicating that people who settled in island of the Philippines (mostly in the Visayas) come from "afar". Malaysia is so named (the original name of Malyasia was "Malaya" – or the land of the Malays).[6] The "orang asli" in Malaysia are Austronesians, bearing genetic and cultural affinity with their brothers and sisters in the Pacific islands – Polynesia, Micronesia, and Melanesia.

Later arrivals in Singapore and Malaysia are "orang asing" or "foreigners" and bear Indian, Chinese and European strains.

In the Philippines, aborigines in Japan (the "Ainus") and from Taiwan were the early settlers. From the Philippines, they stayed for may be a millennium before spreading to the Pacific islands, as far as Hawaii and New Zealand.

---

[6] *"Malaya" in Pilipino means "free".*

Above. The Ainu's of Japan, one of the early ancestors of Austronesians who came to the Philippines, and spread outward to the Pacific islands and became Polynesians, Micronesians and Melanesians. (Photo credit: downloaded from the Internet, Free Public Online Use)

Austronesian Numerals

Table 53: Numerals in Some Representative Austronesian Languages*

	Paiwan	Cebuano	Javanese	Malagasy	Arosi	Hawaiian
'one'	ita	usá	siji	isa	e-ta'i	e-kahi
'two'	dusa	duhá	loro	roa	e-rua	e-lua
'three'	tjelu	tulú	telu	telo	e-oru	e-kolu
'four'	sepatj	upát	papat	efatra	e-hai	e-hā
'five'	lima	limá	lima	dimy	e-rima	e-lima
'six'	unem	unúm	nem	enina	e-ono	e-ono
'seven'	pitju	pitú	pitu	fito	e-biu	e-hiku
'eight'	alu	walú	wolu	valo	e-waru	e-walu
'nine'	siva	siyám	sanga	sivy	e-siwa	e-iwa
'ten'	ta-puluq	púlu'	se-puluh	folo	ta-nga-huru	'umi

*Hyphens separate numerals from prefixed particles that are not shared by all languages.

Note the numbers "5" and "8", "lima" and "walu" – in Table 53, above. They are carried almost intact across Austronesian languages.

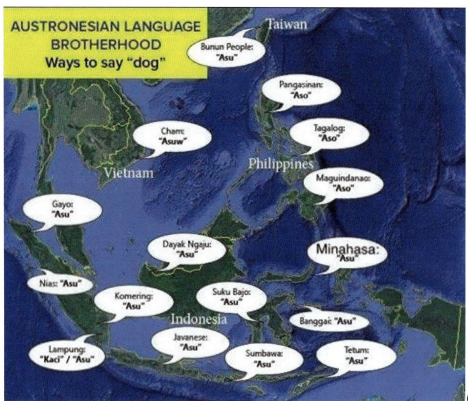

(Photo credit: Tiz Wezza, FB, Pacific Culture cor Filipino Agnostics and Atheists)

"Dog" – "asu" is universally used from Taiwan to Southeast Asia, indicating a common origin of Austronesian peoples.

"Comparison of selected words in Cebuano (Philippines), Kadazan (Borneo), and Melayu (Malaysia)" – see below.

PERBANDINGAN FONETIK BAHASA CEBUANO/VISAYAN FILIPINA – KADAZANDUSN BORNEO DAN BAHASA MELAYU

CEBUANO/VISAYAN – KADAZANDUSN - BAHASA MELAYU

paa	poho	paha
tuhod	totud	lutut
tikod	gontod	tumit
lapalapa	lapap/lukap	tapak kaki
pilak	pirok	perak
tubo	tobu	tebu
bugas	wagas	beras
asin	osin/tusi	garam
moinom	minum	minum
mukaon	makan	makan
baboy	wogok	babi
kanding	kambing	kambing
manok	manuk/piyak	ayam
buhok	tobuk/tokobuk	rambut
kilay	kudou	kirai
mata	mato	mata
ilong	todung	hidung
lalaki	kusai	lelaki
tuba	bahar	tuak

Note the close linguistic rendering of "mata" (eyes), "kambing" (goat), "makan" (eat), "minum" (drink), "tubo" (body or sugar cane), "pilak" (silver – indicating that silver is mined in Austronesian islands), and, ""paa" (feet). The other words are similarly spelled and pronounced.

Micronesia

Spread across the western Pacific Ocean, the Federated States of Micronesia comprises more than 600 islands. It consists of 4 island states: Pohnpei, Kosrae, Chuuk and Yap. The islands, lying low on the Pacific, are known for palm-shaded beaches, wreck-filled dives and ancient ruins, including Nan Madol, sunken basalt temples and burial vaults that extend out of a lagoon on Pohnpei. Capital: Palikir. Currency: United States Dollar. Recognized regional languages: Chuukese; Kosraean; Pohnpeian; Yapese. Population: 104,937 (2016) World Bank. (Google)

(Above) Yapese girl, Micronesia. (Photo credit – Alamy.com - downloaded from the Internet)

(Below) Young girls - Hula dancers, Micronesia. (Photo credit – Alamy.com - downloaded from the Internet)

Part Two - Sketches Of Major Austronesian Locations

Introduction

"The term *Austronesian peoples* refers to a population group present in Southeast Asia or Oceania who speak, or had ancestors who spoke, one of the Austronesian languages. Apart from the Polynesian people of Oceania, the Austronesian people include: Taiwanese Aborigines, the majority ethnic groups of East Timor, Indonesia and Malaysia."

"Western scholars believe the Austronesian people originated on the island of Taiwan following the migration of pre-Austronesian-speaking peoples from continental Asia approximately 10,000-6000 B.C. Due to a lengthy split from the Pre-Austronesian populations, the Proto-Austronesian language; the cultures and ethnic groups of the Austronesian peoples began on Taiwan approximately 6,000 years ago."

"The Austronesian people themselves have a variety of different traditions and history of their origins. According to most Western scholars, however, the Austronesian people originated in the island of Taiwan, and are spread as far away as Madagascar in the Indian Ocean and the Polynesian islands of the Pacific Ocean."

"According to mainstream Western studies, a large scale Austronesian expansion began around 5000-2500 B.C. Population growth primarily fuelled this migration. These first settlers may have landed in northern Luzon in the island of the Philippines intermingling with the earlier Austral-Melanesian population who had inhabited the islands about 23,000 years earlier. Over the next thousand years, the Austronesian people migrated south-east to the rest of the Philippine Islands, and into the islands of the Celebes Sea, Borneo, and Indonesia. The Austronesian people of Maritime Southeast Asia sailed eastward, and spread to the islands of Melanesia and Micronesia between 1200 BE.CO., and 500 A.DO. respectively. The Austronesian inhabitants that spread westward through Maritime Southeast Asia had reached some parts of mainland Southeast Asia, and later on to Madagascar." *(Data source: http://www.ourpacificocean.com/austronesian_people/)*[7]

(Sources of photos/maps/data in this section: online Free Internet Public Use - Country Govt websites, Tour & Hotel operators, and Google/Wikipedia – Nov 2017)

---

[7] *<Austroneisan People> online – Google Search - Polynesian Cultural Center www.Polynesia.com*

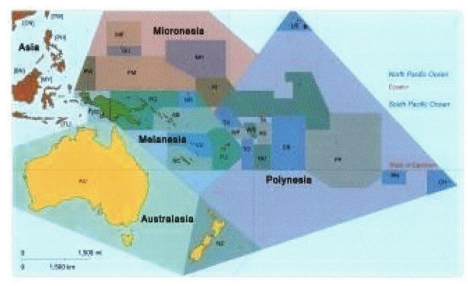
The cultural societies called "Austronesians" are distinct language groups found in Southeast Asia, Oceania and islands adjacent to East Africa whose languages are very closely related, and may be traced to the Austronesian family of languages. Their origins are believed to be Taiwanese aborigines. From this beginning, they now form the majority of ethnic groups in the Philippines, Malaysia, East Timor, Indonesia, Brunei, Cocos (Keeling) Islands, Madagascar, Micronesia, and Polynesia, as well as the Malay people of Singapore. The Polynesian peoples of New Zealand and Hawaii, and the non-Papuan people of Melanesia belong to this larger Austronesian family. They are also found in the regions of the Pattani in Thailand, the Cham areas in Vietnam and Cambodia, and in the Hainan island, China; also in parts of Sri Lanka, southern Myanmar, southern tip of South Africa, Suriname and some of the Andaman Islands. The people of the Maldives has traces of Austronesian believed to have come from the Malay Archipelago. These are known collectively as "Austronesia". *(Data source – downloaded from the Internet, Free Public Use).*

In terms of language, the Austronesian family includes most of the languages spoken in the islands of the Pacific with the exception of the indigenous Papuan and Australian languages. Austronesia includes Madagascar, Indonesia, the Philippines, Taiwan and the Pacific islands of Melanesia, Micronesia and Polynesia. With 1,268 languages, Austronesian is one of the largest and the most geographically far spread language families of the world.

Austronesian languages are spoken in Brunei, Cambodia, Chile, China, Cook Islands, East Timor, Fiji, French Polynesia, Guam, Indonesia, Kiribati, Madagascar, Malaysia, Marshall Islands, Mayotte, Micronesia, Myanmar, Nauru, New Caledonia, New Zealand, Niue, Northern Mariana Islands, Palau, Papua New Guinea, Philippines, Samoa, Solomon Islands, Suriname, Taiwan, Thailand, Tokelau, Tonga, Tuvalu, USA, Vanuatu, Viet Nam, Wallis and Futuna. The total number of speakers of Austronesian languages is estimated at 311,740,132.

The present ASEAN (Association of SouthEast Asian Nations) is a gathering of part of this large group.

(One of the main references used for Part Two, "Sketches . . .", following, is www.bbc.com/news/world-asia-pacific-12990058.)

Brunei Darussalam

Population 413,000 (2015). Area 5,765 sq km (2,226 sq miles). Major languages Malay, English, Chinese. Ethnicity 65% ethnic Malay, 10% Chinese. Religious make-up 78% Muslim, 8% Christian, 7% Buddhist.

Brunei is a small country in Borneo, bordered by Sarawak and Sabah, which are part of Malaysia. Sabah is being claimed by the Philippines, based on a rental document to the Sultan of Sulu, Philippines, to whom the late Sultan of Brunei gave the land in exchange for the armed assistance by Sulu to Brunei to put down an uprising.

The "Sabah Claim" started in the 1970s with Philippine President Marcos. It has not been pursued vigorously, as of this writing (2018). The Kiram Family of Sulu, which yielded sovereignty of the claim to the Philippine government is waiting. The rental is still being paid to the Kiram Family by Malaysia – proof of non-ownership – which supports the Philippine claim to Sabah.

Above. Bandar Seri Begawan, capital of Brunei. (pic & map, below, credit – Travel Guide, Brunei. Internet)

Brunei is a tiny nation on the island of Borneo, in 2 distinct sections surrounded by Malaysia and the South China Sea. It's known for its beaches and biodiverse rainforest, much of it protected within reserves. The capital, Bandar Seri Begawan, is home to the opulent Jame'Asr Hassanil

Bolkiah mosque and its 29 golden domes. The capital's massive Istana Nurul Iman palace is the

residence of Brunei's ruling sultan.

The tiny state of Brunei has one of the world's highest standards of living thanks to its bountiful oil and gas reserves.

Its ruling royals, led by the head of state Sultan Hassanal Bolkiah, possess a huge private fortune and its largely ethnic-Malay population enjoy generous state handouts and pay no taxes.

A British protectorate since 1888, Brunei was the only Malay state in 1963 which chose to remain so rather than join the federation that became Malaysia. Full independence came relatively late in 1984.

Above. Flag of Brunei (pic source: Travel Guide, Brunei, Internet.)

Cambodia – Cham People

The Chams, or Cham people (Cham: *Urang Campa*,Vietnamese: *người Chăm* or *người Chàm*, Khmer), are an ethnic group of Austronesian origin in Southeast Asia. Their contemporary population, a diaspora is concentrated between the Kampong Cham Province in Cambodia and Phan Rang–Tháp Chàm, Phan Thiết, Ho Chi Minh City and An Giang Province in Southern Vietnam. An additional 4,000 Chams live in Bangkok, Thailand, who had migrated during Rama I's reign. Recent immigrants are mainly students and workers, who preferably seek work and education in the southern Islamic Pattani, Narathiwat, Yala, and Songkhla provinces. Cham people represent the core of the Muslim communities in both Cambodia and Vietnam.

Above. Cham children selling at the public market. (Photo credit to <www.cathyand garystravelpages.com>

From the 2nd to the mid-15th century the Chams populated Champa, a contiguous territory of independent principalities in central and southern Vietnam. They spoke the Cham language, a Malayo-Polynesian language of the Austronesian language family. Chams and Malays are the only sizable Austronesian peoples, that had settled in Iron Age Mainland Southeast Asia among the more ancient Austroasiatic inhabitants. *(Data source:* en.wikipedia.org/wiki/Chams).

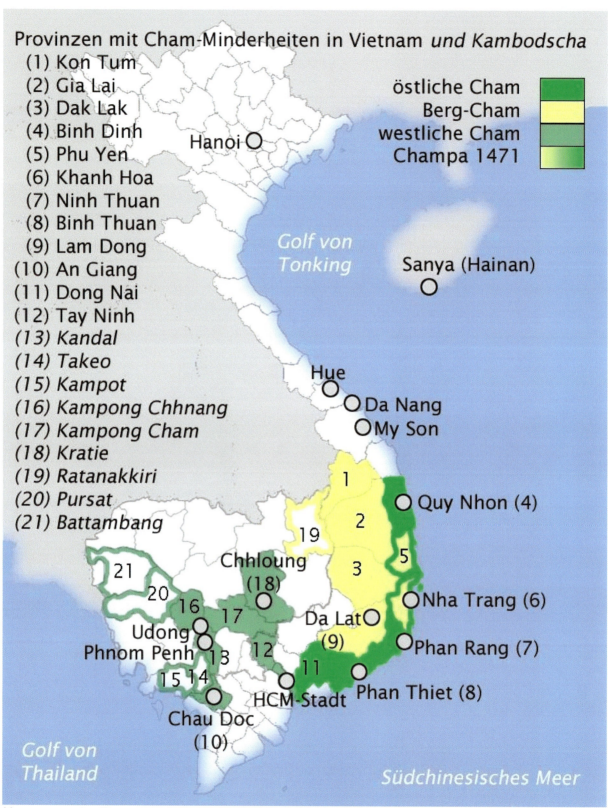

Above, map by Roxanna - based on Map of Ethnic Groups in Indochina 1970 and J.W. Bromlej: (народы мира – историко-этнографический справочник (Moscow 1988),, CC BY-SA 3.0, https://commons.wikimedia.org/w/index.php?curid=12144508)

Austronesian origin, patterns and chronology of migration remain debated and it is assumed, that the Cham people arrived in peninsular Southeast Asia via Borneo. As mainland Southeast Asia had been populated on land routes by members of the Austroasiatic language family, such as the Mon people and the Khmer people around 5,000 years ago, the Chams were accomplished seafarers belonging to the Austronesian marine migrants, that from 4,000 years BP populated and soon dominated maritime Southeast Asia.[12] Earliest known records of Cham presence in Indochina date back to the second century CE.

 *Flag of the FLC – Front de Libération du Champa, which was active during the Vietnam War.* (Editor: The Viet Nam war of independence started from the independence recolution against the French colonialists in the 1930s, to WW2/1939-1941, and ended in April 1975 when the Americans were defeated and evacuated Saigon/Ho Chi Minh city – a long war of about 45 years where millions of Viet Namese died.)

"Austronesians in Cambodia"

(Written by Kristian Ligsay Jensen, FB, and posted in FB to Tiz Wezza and to Emmanuel Ikan Astillero).

"The only Austronesians in Vietnam are the Chams of Southern Vietnam -- centered mostly around the coastal town of Nha Trang."

"The Chams once had a dominant Indianized (Hindu/Buddhist) kingdom, the Kingdom of Champa, in what is today southern Vietnam with a culture very reminiscent of Cambodia, Laos, Thailand, and Myanmar. They were almost completely decimated in the 12th century with successive Vietnamese invasions from the north until they managed to maintain a small enclave in what is today Nha Trang. Many fled to neighboring Cambodia, which had a similar culture, and there are Chams today still living there. They maintained cultural ties with the Malay and a significant portion of them are Muslims today."

(Above) Austronesian *Cham dancers in Cambodia* (Photo credit: Jérémy Couture - originally posted to Flickr as Danses Cham, CC BY 2.0, https://commons.wikimedia.org/w/index.php?curid=5198352)

Cham family – Muslims. Photo credit - Sorinchan Suzana, USAID/Cambodia/PROGD - http://www.usaid.gov/kh/Photos_Archive/photos_archive_good_governance.htm USAID Cambodia website, Public Domain, https://commons.wikimedia.org/w/index.php?curid=2486587

Chile/Rapa Nui or Easter Islands

Polynesians from central Pacific sailed east to Easter Island or Rapa Nui near South America where the well-known Moaui or statues are found.

(Map source: rohrmannspace.net <https://images.search.yahoo.com/search/images?p=map+rapa+nui>

The Easter Island statues (below). The present inhabitants of Rapa Nui are Polynesians. They send cultural delegations to Polynesian festivals, showing their dances which are closely similar to Hawaiian and Tahitian hula dances.

Easter Island's (Rapa Nui) aboriginal population was almost completely lost from European-introduced diseases and by slavers in the 1860s. Chile took sovereignty in 1888, becoming the only Pacific islanders under a Latin American government. The Easter Island original culture vanished. The Polynesian language (also called Rapa Nui) survives. Much archeological studies have been done in the island to determine how the megalith statues were moved from the quarry miles away, where unfinished statues still remain, to the seashore. No explanations have come, so far.

The native Polynesian inhabitants of Easter Island in the Pacific Ocean are the Rapa Nuis. Located at the easternmost of the Pacific Ocean, very much far from Tahiti where the Rapa Nuis may have originated, they carried, to date, a distinct Polynesian culture. They make up about 60% of the current Rapa Nui population and have a significant portion of their population residing in mainland Chile. Their language are the traditional Austronesian-Rapa Nui language and the primary language of Chile, Spanish. At the 2002 census there were 3,304 island inhabitants—almost all living in the village of Hanga Roa on the sheltered west coast. The population is estimated, in 2016, to have reached 5,682. Related ethnic groups are Oparoan, Tahitian.

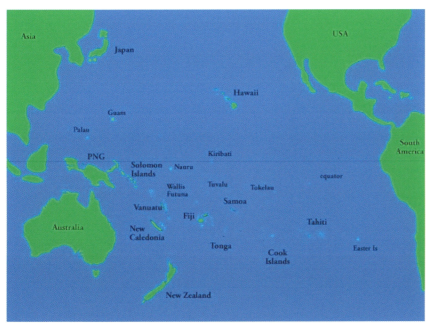

Rapa Nui/Easter Island.
(From Wikipedia, the Free Encyclopedia)

As of 2011, Rapa Nui's main source of income derived from tourism, which focuses on the giant sculptures called Moai.

(From Wikipedia, the free encyclopedia, photo credit: realhistoryww)

Polynesian inhabitants performing at the Rapa Nui National Park . (Photo credit: Chile Travel)

China – Taiwan - Formosa

According to Robert Blust (1999), Austronesian is divided in several primary branches, all but one of which are found exclusively on Taiwan. The Formosan languages of Taiwan are grouped into as many as nine first-order subgroups of Austronesian. All Austronesian languages spoken outside Taiwan (including its offshore Yami language) belong to the Malayo-Polynesian branch,

sometimes called *Extra-Formosan*."Out of Taiwan" model   An Atayal tribal woman from Taiwan with tattoo on her face as a symbol of maturity. (Photo credit: *en.wikipedia.org*)

Pretty Taiwan Yami aborigines. Note the traditional costume which is similar to the Mandaya tribe of Davao, Philippines. (*See Section, below, on the Philippines*.)
https://images.search.yahoo.com/search/images?p=taiwan+aborigines

Iona tribe children – Taiwan aborigines. (Photo credit: *en.wikipedia.org*)

An element in the ancestry of Austronesian-speaking peoples, the one which carried their ancestral language, originated on the island of Taiwan following the migration of pre-Austronesian-speaking peoples from continental Asia between approximately 10,000–6,000 BC.

Other research has suggested that, according to radiocarbon dates, Austronesians may have migrated from mainland China to Taiwan as late as 4000 BC. Before Taiwan, Austronesian speakers are thought to have been descended from the neolithic cultures of Southeastern China, such as the Hemudu culture or the Liangzhu culture. According to the mainstream "out-of-Taiwan model", a large-scale Austronesian expansion began around 5000–2500 BC. Population growth primarily fuelled this migration. These first settlers may have landed in northern Luzon in the archipelago of the Philippines, intermingling with the earlier Australo-Melanesian population who had inhabited the islands since about 23,000 years earlier.

Over the next thousand years, Austronesian peoples migrated southeast to the rest of the Philippines, and into the islands of the Celebes Sea, Borneo, and Indonesia. The Austronesian peoples of Maritime Southeast Asia sailed eastward, and spread to the islands of Melanesia and Micronesia between 1200 BC and 500 AD respectively. The Austronesian inhabitants that spread westward through Maritime Southeast Asia had reached some parts of mainland Southeast Asia, and later on Madagascar. *(Data source: Wiki – the Free Encyclopedia)*

Taiwan aboriginal dancers. (Photo credit – www.taipics.com https://images.search.yahoo.com/search/images)

Linguistic and archaeological evidence identify Taiwan as the origin of the initial dispersal of Austronesian languages. This occurred many centuries after Neolithic settlers introduced grain agriculture, pottery making, and domesticated animals to the island from the adjacent mainland of China about 4000 BCE. About 3500 BCE, groups with a cultural resemblance to those in Taiwan appeared in the northern Philippines. After another millennium these cultural practices and customs appeared also in Indonesia islands. The etymological traces suggest a southward and eastward movement from Island Southeast Asia (ISEA) to Austronesian –speaking groups around the northern coast of New Guinea. They, then, moved to western Pacific a millennium later. From New Guinea and the Bismarck Archipelago, these people spread out, using sturdy ocean-sailing outrigger canoes containing whole communities. There is a thousand-year gap before the settlement of central and eastern Polynesia. Hawaii and New Zealand were settled from central Pacific (Tahiti) lately within the past 1,500–1,700 years. *(Data source: "Austronesian Languages" - Encyclopedia Britannica in the Net, from Google site – For Free Public Use).*

Taiwan Aborigines – Bunun Tribe. (Photo credit – www.flickr.com on the net)

"Formosan language" is a collective term for a highly diverse collection of languages, most of which share broad typological similarities with languages in the Philippines and some other areas (such as Madagascar). The Yami language, which is spoken on Lan-yü (Botel Tobago) island off the southeastern coast of Taiwan, forms a subgroup with Ivatan and Itbayaten in the northern Philippines. The other 14 surviving aboriginal languages of Taiwan may fall into as many as six primary branches of the language family, each one coordinate with the entire Malayo-Polynesian branch. Under such circumstances very small subgroups or even single languages provide an independent line of evidence for the nature of Proto-Austronesian that is theoretically equivalent to the entire Malayo-Polynesian branch of some 1,180 member languages. Among the best-described Formosan languages are Atayal (spoken in the northern mountains), Amis (spoken along the narrow east coast), and Paiwan (spoken near the southern tip of the island). *(Data source: Google – Free Public Use in the Internet – see: "Austronesian Languages" - Encyclopedia Britannica in the Net).*

Cook Islands

Capital: Avarua, on Rarotonga. Status Self-governing territory in free association with New Zealand . Population 15,600. Area 237 sq km (91 sq miles). Major languages English and Cook Islands Maori. Major religion Christianity

The 15 volcanic islands and coral atolls of the Cook Islands are scattered over 770,000 square miles of the South Pacific, between American Samoa to the west and French Polynesia to the east.

The 15 islands in the Cooks are located in the heart of the Pacific, halfway between Hawaii and New Zealand. (www.cookislands.travel)

Map source: Air New Zealand, online, advertisement.

A former British protectorate which became self-governing in 1965, the territory is now in free association with New Zealand.

Its economy centres on tourism; the territory's natural assets include fine beaches and volcanic mountains.

Named after Captain Cook, who explored them in 1773, the islands were once autonomous, home to tribes of mixed Polynesian ancestry.

Above. A Cook Islands resort. Note the "nipa hut" architectural style common all over the Pacific Austronesians, including the Philippines, Indonesia and Malaysia. (Photo credit, guidetropical.com)

Governments still seek advice on matters of culture, custom and land ownership from a council of hereditary leaders known as the House of Ariki.

More than twice as many native Cook Islanders live in New Zealand than live in the islands themselves. Most of them have left in search of a brighter economic future. As New Zealand citizens they can also live in Australia.

Black pearls are the chief export. Agriculture, the sale of fishing licences to foreign fleets and offshore finance are also key revenue earners.

The Cook Islands is a self-governing island country in the South Pacific Ocean in free association with New Zealand. It comprises 15 islands whose total land area is 240 square kilometres .(Data Source: cook-islands.gov.ck) . Capital: Avarua. Currency: New Zealand dollar (NZD). Population: 17,600. The lush green island of Rarotonga, ringed by white-sand beaches, and the stunning coral atoll of Aitutaki (with its blue lagoon), epitomizes the beauty of the Cook Islands, and for that matter, all of Polynesia.

Above. Miss Cook Islands, 2017 (Pic credit, Joey Miguel, FB-Pacific Culture... Oct 2017)

East Timor – Timor Leste

Official Name: Republika Demokratika Timor Loro Sa'e [Tetum]; Republica Democratica de Timor-Leste [Portuguese] ; short form: Timor Loro Sa'e [Tetum]; Timor-Leste [Portuguese]; conventional long form: Democratic Republic of Timor-Leste; conventional short form: East Timor.

Above pic – Tutuala Los Palos Area, Timor Leste - 22 Dec 2007. (Photo credit: martineperret.photoshelter.com)

Timor-Leste, also known as East Timor, is a relative new nation, in the eastern half of the island of Timor, at the eastern 'end' of the Lesser Sunda Islands, north of the Timor Sea and Australia. The country is bordered by Indonesia in west and the Savu Sea in north.

Map from the UN Security Council Resolution (downloaded from Google Free Public Use, Online)

The country occupies an area of 14,874 km², including the islands of Pulau Atauro and Paula Jaco, and an enclave, Pante Makasar, within West Timor (Inonesia). It is about half the size of Belgium, or slightly larger than the Bahamas.

Above. Dili girls in traditional costume. (Photo credit: Chief Minister, Treasury & Economic Development Directorate, Timor Leste, posted in FB)

The nation has a population of 1.2 million people (in 2015), capital and largest city is Dili, spoken languages are Tetuma and Portuguese (both official), Indonesian, English. *(Data Source: One World Nations Online - http://www.nationsonline.org/oneworld/timor_leste.htm)*

Loy Krathong dance – Timor Leste – (Photo credit – thingsasian.com < https://www.google.com.ph/search?q=timor+leste>)

Most of the people are of Papuan, Malayan, and Polynesian origin and are predominantly Christian. About 40 different Papuan and Malayan languages or dialects are spoken, dominated by Tetum. Portuguese is spoken by a small fraction of the population, but it is one of the country's two official languages, the other being Tetum; Indonesian and English are considered to be "working" languages. *(Data source: Google Search: Free Public Use, see - Encyclopedia Britannica Online)*

Fiji

Capital: Suva.   Currency: Fiji dollar (FJD).   Population: 818,100 (2015).   Area: 18,274 km².

Fiji's main island is known as Viti Levu and it is from this that the name "Fiji" is derived, though the common English pronunciation is based on that of Fiji - officially the Republic of Fiji (Fijian: *Matanitu Tugalala o Viti*) is an island country in Melanesia in the South Pacific Ocean about 1,100 nautical miles (2,000 km; 1,300 mi) northeast of New Zealand's North Island. Its closest neighbours are Vanuatu to the west, New Caledonia to the southwest, New Zealand's Kermadec Islands to the southeast, Tonga to the east, the Samoas and France's Wallis and Futuna to the northeast, and Tuvalu to the north.

Above. Fijians at Raviravi Island. (pic credit: readtiger.com - https://images.search.yahoo.com/search)

Fiji is an archipelago of more than 330 islands, of which 110 are permanently inhabited, and more than 500 islets, amounting to a total land area of about 18,300 square kilometres

(7,100 sq mi). The farthest island is Ono-i-Lau. The two major islands, Viti Levu and Vanua Levu, account for 87% of the total population of 898,760. The capital, Suva on Viti Levu, serves as Fiji's principal cruise port About three-quarters of Fijians live on Viti Levu's coasts, either in Suva or in smaller urban centres like Nadi (tourism) or Lautoka (sugar cane industry). Viti Levu's interior is sparsely inhabited due to its terrain. *(data source: en.wikipedia.org/wiki/Fiji)*

The majority of Fiji's islands were formed through volcanic activity starting around 150 million years ago. Today, some geothermal activity still occurs on the islands of Vanua Levu and Taveuni. Fiji has been inhabited since the second millennium BC, and was settled first by Austronesians and later by Melanesians, with some Polynesian influences. Europeans visited Fiji from the 17th century, and, after a brief period as an independent kingdom, the British established the Colony of Fiji in 1874. Fiji was a Crown colony until 1970, when it gained independence as a Commonwealth realm. A republic was declared in 1987. (Wikipedia)

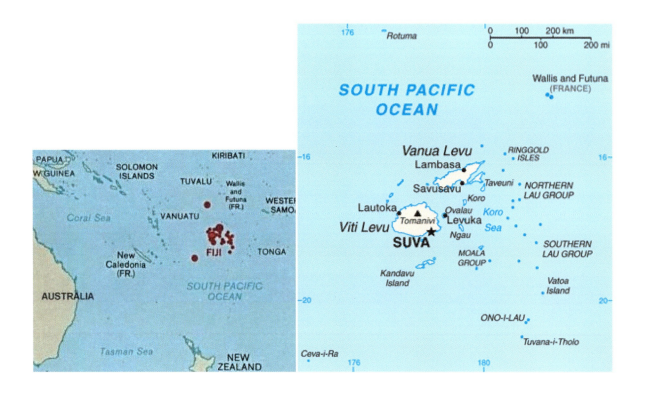

(Map credit: Central Intelligence Agency - ttp://www.lib.utexas.edu/maps/islands_oceans_poles/fiji.jpg, Public Domain, *https://commons.wikimedia.org/w/index.php?curid=6627221*)

Above. Fijian dancers before start of program. (pic credit: By Julie Lyn from Washington, DC, USA - FijiUploaded by AlbertHerring, CC BY 2.0, https://commons.wikimedia.org/w/index.php?curid=29238510)

French Polynesia

  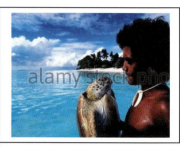

www.worldatlas.com/webimage/flags/countrys/pacific/frenchpy.htm (Photos – Alamy.com)

French Polynesia, an overseas collectivity of France, comprises more than 100 islands in the South Pacific, stretching for more than 2,000km. Divided into the Austral, Gambier, Marquesas, Society and Tuamotu archipelagos, they're known for their coral-fringed lagoons and over-the-water bungalow hotels. Island features include white- and black-sand beaches, mountains, rugged backcountry and towering waterfalls. Capital: Papeete; Currency: Ethnic groups (2015): 78% Polynesians; 12% Chinese; 6% French Polynesian; 4% French. *(Data source: Google - https://www.google.com.ph).*

Tahitian girls – French Polynesia. (Photo credit: Orion Tahiti Cruise - https://www.google.com.ph/search?q=french+polynesia+people+images)

Of the many islands in the Pacific, it is believed that French Polynesia was one of the last settled by Austronesians. Scientists hold that the Great Polynesian Migration happened around 1500 BC as Austronesian people went on a journey using celestial navigation to find islands in the South Pacific Ocean. The first islands of French Polynesia to be settled were the Marquesas Islands in about 200 BC. The Polynesians later ventured southwest and discovered the Society islands around AD 300. *(Google Online)*

Bora Bora resort, French Polynesia. (Photo credit: Kiwi Collection.)

Tahitian dancers- French Polynesia. (Photo credit: sca.france.fr online https://www.google.com.ph/search?q=french+polynesia)

Guam and Northern Mariana Islands

Guamanian flag.
(Photo credit: guampedia)

According to the 2000 Census, approximately 65,000 people of Chamorro ancestry live on Guam and another 19,000 live in the Northern Marianas. Another 93,000 live outside the Marianas in Hawaii and the West Coast of the United States. The Chamorros are primarily Austronesian, but many also have European and East Asian ancestry. (Google search)

Above photo of Chamorro Festival Dancers in Saipan. (Photo credit: flickriver.com - https://www.google.com.ph/search?q=chamorro+people+images)

Chamorro people. The Chamorro people are the indigenous people of the Mariana Islands; politically divided between the United States territory of Guam and the United States Commonwealth of the Northern Mariana Islands in Micronesia. *(Data source: Chamorro people - Wikipedia; https://en.wikipedia.org/wiki/Chamorro_people)*

Tao-Tao Tano: "People of the Land" (Photo credit: Tasithoughts.Weblog - https://www.google.com.ph/search?q=chamorro+people+images)

Chamorro is an Austronesian language spoken by about 47,000 people. It is the native and spoken language of the Chamorro people who are the indigenous people of Guam and the Northern Mariana Islands, US territories. *(Wikipedia - Language family: Austronesian languages, Malayo-Polynesian languages).*

Chamorro dance – Pa'a Tao-Tao Tano (photo credit Guampedia. https://www.google.com.ph/search?q=chamorro+people)

During the Spanish Colonial Era, the Chamoru population was greatly reduced by the introduction of European diseases and changes in society under Spanish rule. The Spanish killed many Chamoru men and relocated most others to Guam, where they lived in several parishes to prevent rebellion. Some[who?] estimate that as many as 100,000 Chamorus may have populated the Marianas when Europeans first settled in 1667. By 1800, there were under 10,000. Within the parishes, the Spanish eventually focused their efforts on converting the natives to Catholicism. Father Frances X. Hezel stated that Chamorus caught or reported engaging in pagan "sorcery" were publicly punished. Through this, they were given Spanish surnames through Catálogo Alfabético de Apellidos or Alphabetic Catalog of Surnames. Thus, a multiracially mixed Chamorro with European descent and a Spanish surname may not necessarily have Spanish blood, any more than Filipinos with Spanish surnames do. (Data source: https://en.wikipedia.org/wiki/Chamorro_people)

Above photo – Young Chamorro dancers doing the Polynesian grass skirt hula. Note that the grass skirt dancing is common from Hawaii to New Zealand, to Easter Islands in Chile. (photo from Guampdn.com - https://www.google.com.ph/search?q=chamorro+people).

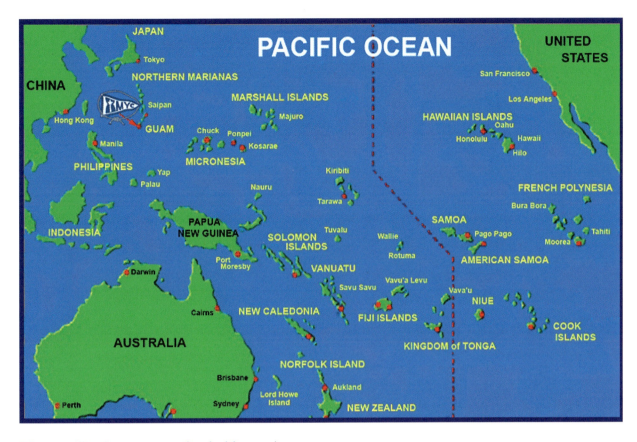

(Map credit, above, www.pinsdaddy.com)

(Seal and pic, above, from Google Search, "Free to Use" images)

"Religious Beliefs of Guam"

Guam was invaded and conquered by Spanish soldiers and missionized by Catholic priests. Beginning in 1668, making the island the first Pacific outpost of European colonization and religion. All the Chamorro People from Guam and the neighboring islands were forcibly resettled into mission villages. Within the first forty years of Spanish missionization on Guam, the Chamorro people suffered catastrophic depopulation, losing perhaps 90 percent of their population to disease, warfare, and the hardships brought about by resettlement and forced labor on plantations. Protestant and Catholic missions were established elsewhere throughout the Micronesian islands during the mid-1800s, and a similar pattern of depopulation from introduced diseases ensued on Yap, Pohnpei, and other Micronesian Islands. All of the larger islands of Micronesia have been Christianized for at least a century, and in no place was local resistance successfully maintained for very long. Chamorros today are nearly entirely Roman Catholic, while in other areas of Micronesia, Protestants slightly outnumber Catholics.

During the past twenty years a number of Christian sects have gained a small foothold, including Baptists, Mormons, Seventh-Day Adventists, and Jehovah's Witnesses. In Guam, Catholic beliefs and practices are heavily flavored with elements from Filipino animism and spiritualism, indigenous Chamorro ancestor veneration, and medieval European idolizing of religious icons. Elsewhere in Micronesia, there is a similar syncretic mix of modern Christian theology and practice with indigenous beliefs in animism and many varieties of magic. *(Text source: Tiz Wezza,, FB, 17/11/2017 - Filipino Agnostics and Atheists Against Cultural Marxism;* Read more: http://www.everyculture.com/.../Micronesians-Religion-and-Exp...)

Catholic Church believers in procession in Agahan (Agana) Guam. (Photo credit: Tiz Wezza, FB, sent to the author.

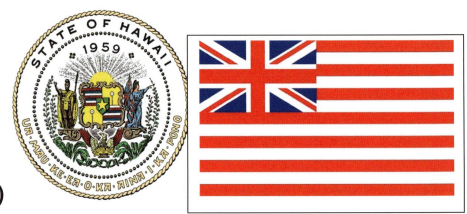

Hawaii (U.S.A.)

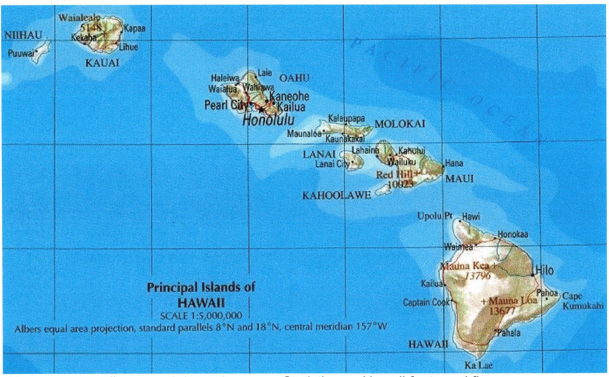

(Above, map credit: *www.statemaster.com* – Statistics on Hawaii facts and figures- https://images.search.yahoo.com/search/images?p=hawaii+people+images.)

15,000 years ago - Polynesians arrive in Hawaii after navigating the ocean using only the stars to guide them. In 1778, Captain James Cook landed at Waimea Bay on the island of Kauai, he was the first European to make contact with the Hawaiian Islands – which he named "Sandwich Islands" after the Earl of Sandwich, U.K. (Data from < *https://www.gohawaii.com/hawaiian-culture/history*>

A Brief History of the Hawaiian People (University of Hawaii), written by W.D. Alexander, 1891, says that due to the "prevailing winds and currents (are) from east and northeast to south and southwest", and tracing oral traditions, songs, chants, etc. – a series of migrations came from central Pacific to Hawaii. Scattered over 4,000 miles of open sea, the Polynesians "speak dialects of the same language (Austronesian - *EIA*), have the same physical features, the same manners and customs, the same general system of tabus, and similar traditions and religious rites." *(Chapt 2, p. 18 – digitized by Google)*

1878 - A Declining Population. When Captain Cook arrived in Hawaii in 1778 there were between 300,000 and 400,000 native Hawaiians, the kanaka maoli. Over the course of the next century the native Hawaiian population dropped between 80-90%. By 1878, the native population was estimated to be between 40,000 and 50,000 people. This decline was due, in large part, to the diseases introduced by contact with foreigners, e.g., venereal disease, small pox, measles, whooping cough and influenza. (Data from: https://www.tripsavvy.com/people-of-hawaii-1529656)

2016 - Pure Hawaiians a Rarity. Over the last 120 years, the numbers of pure Hawaiians, a dying race, have continued to decline. Today, there are less than 8,000 pure Hawaiians alive. As of the 2010 U.S. Census, there were 1,360,301 people living in Hawaii. Of those people, 24.7% were Caucasian, 14.5% were of Filipino descent, 13.6% were of Japanese descent, 8.9% were of Hispanic or Latino descent, 5.9% were of Hawaiian descent and 4.0% were of Chinese descent. *(Data from: https://www.tripsavvy.com/people-of-hawaii-1529656)*

1898: Hawaii was annexed by the United States through the Newlands Resolution. 1900: The Organic Act established the Territory of Hawaii. *(Data source: "The Hawaiian Islands"* https://www.gohawaii.com/hawaiian-culture/history).

Hawaiian "Tiki" totems. (Photo credit – Tiz Wezza, FB-Pacific Culture - *op.cit.* Oct. 2017).

TIKI

- Hawaiian Tiki statues represent the many Tiki gods in Hawaiian and Polynesian mythology. They are carved from wood or stone and are most common in Central Eastern Polynesia. The original Tiki statues were carved by skilled artisans in the Maori tribe, which inhabited the islands until the early 1800s. The statues each have a distinct look that relates to the symbolic meaning and mythological importance of a particular deity.

Hula Dancers – Waikiki Beachfront Resorts. Hula grass skirt dancing – common to Austronesian groups in the Pacific – *Photo credit - www.royal-hawaiian,com:*
https://images.search.yahoo.com/search/images?p=hawaii+people+images

 Hawaiian girl. (Photo credit: *www.royal-hawaiian,com*)

Daguerreotype of the Kamehameha royal family of Hawaii, ca. 1853. Left to right: Kamehameha III (center) and his wife, Queen Kalama (right); Kamehameha IV (right rear), Kamehameha V (left rear) and their sister, Victoria Kamamalu (left).

The last royal family of Hawaii before the take-over of the U.S.A. www.eurweb.com https://images.search.yahoo.com/search/images?p=hawaii+people+image (note: the photo is a negative, and left to right is reversed).

Hawaiian male hula dancers – pic credit from <merriemonarch.staradvertiser.com>
https://images.search.yahoo.com/search/images?p=hawaii+people+images

Hawaiian children hula dancers (Pic from ohfact.com)
https://images.search.yahoo.com/search/images?p=hawaii+people

Waikiki Beach, Ouahu Island, Hawaii. (Pic credit: "djluizmaniac.blogspot.com"
https://images.search.yahoo.com/search/images?p=hawaii+people+images

Indonesia

At 1,904,569 square kilometres (735,358 square miles), Indonesia is the world's 14th-largest country in terms of land area and world's 7th-largest country in terms of combined sea and land area. It has an estimated population of over 261 million people (2015) and is the world's fourth most populous country, the most populous Austronesian nation, as well as the most populous Muslim-majority country. The world's most populous island, Java, contains more than half of the country's population. Capital: Jakarta. Currency: Indonesian rupiah (IDR).

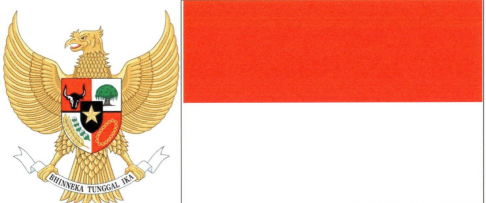Indonesian flag.
Indonesian official seal

*Burubudor Templ.*

Bugis ships. (Two Pics, above, credit – downloaded from the Internet - Wikipedia)

Fossils and the remains of tools show that the Indonesian archipelago was inhabited by *Homo erectus*, known as "Java Man", between 1.5 million years ago and 35,000 years ago. *Homo sapiens* reached the region by around 45,000 years ago. Austronesian peoples, who form the majority of the modern population, migrated to Southeast Asia from Taiwan. They arrived in Indonesia around 2000 BCE, and as they spread through the archipelago, confined the indigenous Melanesian peoples to the far eastern regions. *(Data source: Wikipedia)*

Above. Dancers in Watublapi, Flores, in traditional costume. (Pic credit - Spencer Weart - Own work, CC BY-SA 3.0, https://commons.wikimedia.org/w/index.php?curid=20787593)

Above. Balinese temple dancers. (pic credit: ww.balitourismboard.org)

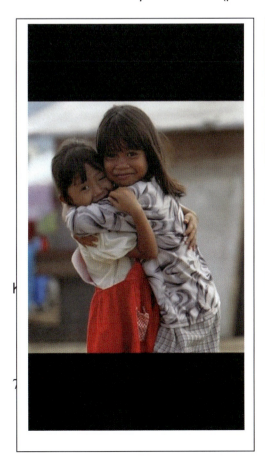

Children of Banda Aceh, Indonesia (Pic credit – Joey Miguel, FB.)

Kiribati

Flag and Coat of Arms

Kiribati - officially the Republic of Kiribati (Gilbertese: *Ribaberiki Kiribati*), is a sovereign state in the central Pacific Ocean. The permanent population is just over 110,000 (2015), more than half of whom live on Tarawa Atoll. The nation comprises 33 atolls and reef islands and one raised coral island, Banaba. They have a total land area of 800 square kilometres (310 sq mi)[12] and are dispersed over 3.5 million square kilometres (1.3 million square miles). Their spread straddles both the equator and the 180th meridian, although the International Date Line goes round Kiribati and swings far to the east, almost reaching the 150°W meridian. This brings the Line Islands into the same day as the Kiribati Islands. Kiribati's easternmost islands, the southern Line Islands, south of Hawaii, have the most advanced time on Earth: UTC+14 hours.
(Data source: Government of Kiribati)

Above. Kiribati Tarawa Atoll, the national capital. (Photo credit – Government of Kiribati.)

The area now called Kiribati has been inhabited by Micronesians speaking the same Oceanic Austronesian language since sometime between 3000 BC and AD 1300. The area was not isolated; invaders from Samoa, Tonga, and Fiji, later introduced Polynesian and Melanesian cultural aspects, respectively. Intermarriage tended to blur cultural differences and resulted in a significant degree of cultural homogenisation.

I-Kiribati children in South Tarawa. (Photo taken by Government of Kiribati employee in the course of their work - Government of Kiribati, posted online for free public use.)

Kiribati young women. (Photo credit: Government of Kiribati, posted online for free public use.

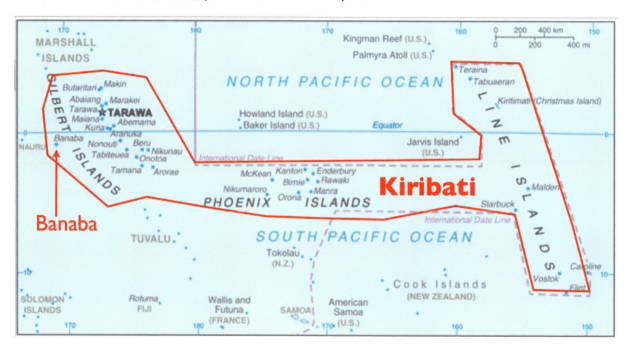

(Above Map & Photo Credit: Government of Kiribati)

Kiribati became independent from the United Kingdom in 1979. The capital and now most populated area, South Tarawa, consists of a number of islets, connected by a series of causeways. These comprise about half the area of Tarawa Atoll.

Kiribati young dancers. Note the hula grass skirts similar to all Austronesian groups throughout the Pacific . (Photo credit – Government of Kiribati – Internet, free public use)

Madagascar

(Map credit: historia con mapas < Seal and Flag - from <MADAMAGAZINE>Siegel

Madagascar (formerly "Malagasy") is the westernmost Austronesian country, if reckoned from Taiwan and the Philippines, from where the original inhabitants of Madagascar came from, sailing via Indonesia.

President: Hery Rajaonarimampianina (2014); Prime Minister: Jean Ravelonarivo (2015); Land area: 224,533 sq mi (581,540 sq km); total area: 226,656 sq mi (587,040 sq km); Population (2014 est.): 23,201,926 (growth rate: 2.62%); birth rate: 33.12/1000; infant mortality rate: 44.88/1000; life expectancy: 65.2' Capital and largest city (2011 est.): Antananarivo, 1.987 million; Monetary unit: Malagasy franc

Madagascar map credit: www.csmeltrophy.co.uk https://images.search.yahoo.com/search/images; (Photo credit, above, right: *Science Online*)

The Malagasy are of mixed Malayo-Indonesian and African-Arab ancestry. Indonesians are believed to have migrated to the island about 700 BCE. (https://www.infoplease.com/country/madagascar).

Malagasy boat that could have sailed from Indonesia to Madagascar. (Photo from: *www.snipview.com https://images.search.yahoo.com/search/images* **- Note the similarity of the Philippine-Austronesian "Balangay Boat" (see "Philippines"**

"Sailing from Melanesia and Micronesia, the Austronesian people discovered Polynesia by 1000 BE.CO. These people settled most of the Pacific Islands. In the Indian Ocean, sailing west from Maritime Southeast Asia. the Austronesian people reached Madagascar by 200 A.D."[8]

"Archaeological evidence suggests that Madagascar was uninhabited until about 1500 or 2000 years ago, when the first Indo-Malayan settlers arrived in coast-hugging craft that skirted the Indian Ocean. They brought traditions such as planting rice in terraced paddies, Southeast Asian food crops and linguistic roots buried in the subcontinent. The migration accelerated in the 9th century, when the powerful Hindu-Sumatran empire of Srivijaya controlled much of the maritime trade in the Indian Ocean." (https://www.lonelyplanet.com/madagascar/history)

Above. Rice terraces in Madagascar.

See Banaue rice terraces, Mt. Province, Philippines.

(Photo fr.https://images.search.yahoo.com/search/images)

Ancient crop remains record epic migration to Madagascar
By Andrew LawlerMay. 30, 2016 , 3:00 PM, Science Online - "The settlement of the Indian Ocean's largest island is one of the great mysteries in humanity's colonization of the globe. Madagascar lies just 400 kilometers off the East African coast. Yet the Malagasy people's cuisine, rituals, and religious beliefs resemble those of Borneo, some 9000 kilometers to the east. Their language is more closely related to Hawaiian than to Bantu, and about half their genes can be traced to Austronesia—that is, Indonesia and the islands of the Pacific. Archaeological evidence of this distant connection was lacking, however."

"New studies trace a wave of Austronesian colonization between 700 C.E. and 1200 C.E. The telltale evidence is, in effect… crops distinctive to Austronesia, sprinkled across Madagascar and neighboring islands. "We finally have a signal of this Austronesian expansion," said Nicole Boivin, an archaeologist and director of the Max Planck Institute for the Science of Human History in Jena, Germany..." - Data source: http://www.sciencemag.org/news/2016/05/ancient-crop-remains-record-epic-migration-madagascar

---

[8] *Austronesian Peoples <http://www.ourpacificocean.com/austronesian_people/>*Polynesian Cultural Center www.Polynesia.com

Selected Events: Political History (Data source: http://www.wildmadagascar.org/history/)

☐ 160 million years ago - Madagascar is born as it separates from the African mainland; ☐ 80 million years ago - Madagascar breaks away from India; ☐ Around 2000 years ago - Madagascar settled by Indonesians or people of mixed Indonesian/African descent.

☐ 1810-1828 - Radama I, a Merina king who has help from the British, unifies most of the country save for the Sakalava kingdom in the far west and far south. Radama opens the country to English missionaries who spread Christianity throughout the island and transcribed Malagasy to a written language. Under his reign, a miniature Industrial Revolution brings induatry to the island. ☐ 1828-1861 - Radama I is succeeded by his widow Ranavalona I, who terrorizes the country for 33 years by persecuting Christians, evicting foreigners, executing political rivals, and reviving the custom of killing babies born on unlucky days.

Above, political rally in Antananarivo. (Photo credit: www.irinnews.org <https://images.search.yahoo.com/search/images>

- 2001 - Marc Ravalomanana, mayor of Tana, is elected president with 52% of the vote. Ratsiraka, the incumbent president, refuses to accept the result and a political trouble ensues. Ratsiraka sets up a a rival government in his home town of Toasmasina and his supporters lay seige to Antananarivo, blocking roads and dynamiting bridges. The population in Tana suffered greatly -- prices for food and vital supplies soared, thousands of jobs were lost, businesses went under, the poor starved. After a court monitored recount reaffirmed that Ravalomanana was indeed the victor, the army lent its support and other nations recognized the elected president's government. Ratsiraka fled in exile to France in July 2002.

- 2006 - Marc Ravalomanana was re-elected for a second term.

- 2009 - President Marc Ravalomanana was ousted in March 2009 during an uprising led by Andry Rajoelina, then-mayor of Antananarivo. Rajoelina has since ushered in a Fourth Republic and rules Madagascar as the President of the High Transitional Authority without recognition from the international community.

"Madagascar Beauties"

Madagascar Austronesians (Photo credit, both pics, above – Tiz Wezza, FB-Pacific Culture – op.cit . .)

Malaysia

Kuala Lumpur City

Malaysian Austronesians

Malaysia is a Southeast Asian country occupying parts of the Malay Peninsula and the island of Borneo. It's known for its beaches, rainforests and mix of Malay, Chinese, Indian and European cultural influences. The capital, Kuala Lumpur, is home to colonial buildings, busy shopping districts such as Bukit Bintang and skyscrapers such as the iconic, 451m-tall Petronas Twin Towers. Capital: Kuala Lumpur. (Data source: https://www.google.com/search?q=malaysia).

(https://en.wikipedia.org/wiki/Malaysia)

Malaysia is a federal constitutional monarchy located in Southeast Asia. It consists of thirteen states and three federal territories and has a total landmass of 330,803 square kilometres (127,720 sq mi) separated by the South China Sea into two similarly sized regions, Peninsular *Malaysia* and East *Malaysia*.

"*Bahasa Melayu*" is the major language of the Austronesian family is widely spoken in Brunei, Indonesia, Malaysia and Singapore. Its users number about 290 million people, located across the Strait of Malacca, the coasts of the Malay Peninsula, and the eastern coast of Sumatra in neighboring Indonesia. It is accepted and used as a native language of part of western coastal Sarawak and West Kalimantan in Borneo. It is the trading language in the southern Philippines, the southern parts of the Zamboanga Peninsula, the Sulu Archipelago and the southern predominantly Muslim-inhabited municipalities of Bataraza and Balabac in Palawan. *(Data source: Wikipedia)*

(Below) Malaysian Austronesians ("orang asli") are predominantly Muslim. (Photo credit – downloaded from the Internet, Free Public Use)

Orang Asli (lit. "original people", "natural people" or "aboriginal people" in Malay) are the indigenous people of Peninsular Malaysia. Officially, there are 18 Orang Asli tribes, categorised under three main groups according to their different languages and customs: 1. Negrito, generally confined to the northern portion of the peninsula
* Kensiu ,Kintak ,Lanoh ,Jahai ,Mendriq, Bateq; 2. Senoi, residing in the central region , *Temiar ,Semai ,Semoq Beri ,Jah Hut, Mahmeri , Che Wong; 3. Proto-Malay (or Aboriginal Malay), in the southern region. *Orang Kuala ,Orang Kanaq ,Orang Seletar ,Jakun ,Semelai ,Temuan

The Semang and Senoi groups, being Austroasiatic-speaking, are the autochthonous (of an inhabitant of a place) peoples of the Malay Peninsula. The Proto-Malays, who speak Austronesian languages, migrated to the area between 2500 and 1500 BC. (Data source - Tiz Wezza, FB, Nov 2 2017. #malaysiatrulyasia #malaysia #orangasli hhmy)

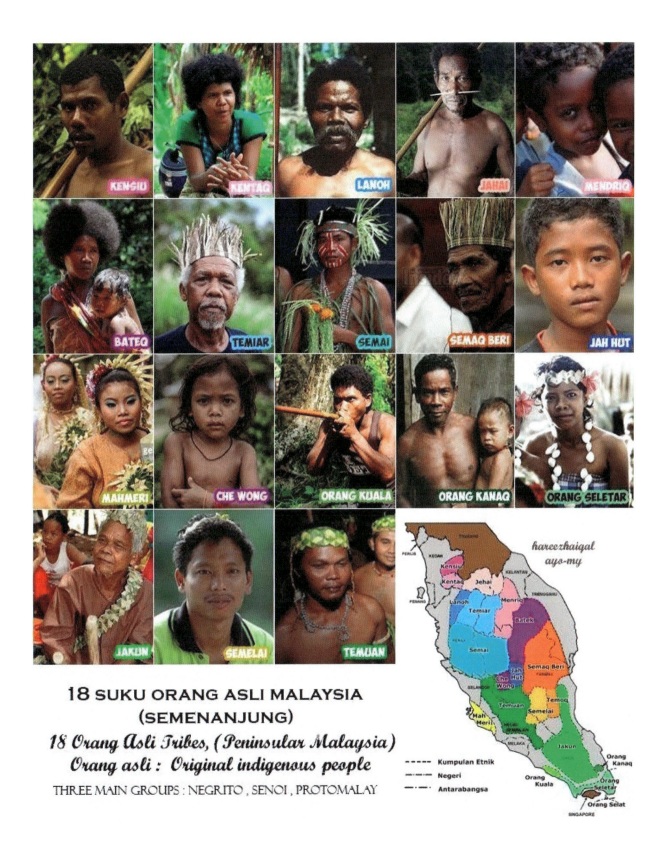

(Below) "Muah Meris", an Austronesian group in Selangor, Malysia. (Photo credit – downloaded from the Internet, Free Online Public Use)

Malaysia is a federation of several autonomous states, each headed by its own sultan – a family hereditary ruler. A parliament is elected from each and sits to make laws, subject to the approval of the sultans and of the supreme sultan.

"Austronesian Sea Dwellers (Orang Laut)"

The sea gypsies or "Orang Laut are a nomadic stateless Austronesian people who's home is the sea resulting in many giving them the label, "sea gypsy". The Orang Laut mostly sail around Singapore, peninsular Malaysia and the Riau islands however they are also known to sail to the Andaman Islands of India.

Interestingly, the Orang Laut still speak an older pure dialect of Malay and still write using the Jawi Arabic script (اورڠ لاوت), this is due to them being isolated and away from the Malay mainland during colonization. (Text and photos from Tiz Wezza, FB, Nov 2017)

(Photo credit – downloaded from the Internet – Free Public Use)

Marshall Islands

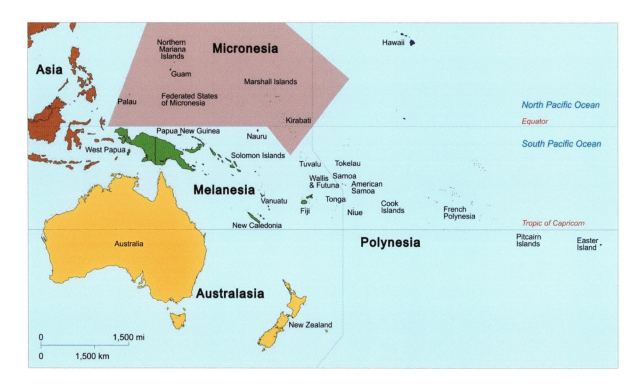

Above, Map credit: "palaudiveadventures.com"
<https://images.search.yahoo.com/search/images?p=marshall+island>

The republic of the Marshall Island an island country found in the northern Pacific Ocean. The country's nearest neighbor is Australia continent a couple of kilometers to the north east. As part of the Micronesia archipelago, the Marshall Islands is made up 34 low-lying coral atolls which in turn are made up of 1156 individual islands and islets. The Marshall Islands' scattered atolls and remote islands supports a population of about 70 thousand people and is far-famed for its marine life and deep sea diving opportunity.

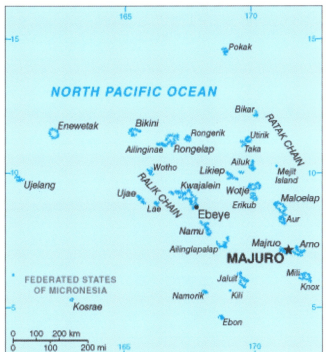 Map credit: Central Intelligence Agency-The World Factbook, online < *https://www.cia.gov/library/publications/the-world-factbook/geos/rm.html*>

 Flag Description

Blue with two stripes radiating from the lower hoist-side corner - orange (top) and white; a white star with four large rays and 20 small rays appears on the hoist side above the two stripes; blue represents the Pacific Ocean, the orange stripe signifies the Ralik Chain or sunset and courage, while the white stripe signifies the Ratak Chain or sunrise and peace; the star symbolizes the cross of Christianity, each of the 24 rays designates one of the electoral districts in the country and the four larger rays highlight the principal cultural centers of Majuro, Jaluit, Wotje, and Ebeye; the rising diagonal band can also be interpreted as representing the equator, with the star showing the archipelago's position just to the north. *World Factbook, online <https://www.cia.gov/library/publications/the-world-factbook/geos/rm.html>*

Young Marshallese women wearing the flag. (Photo credit: "rmimissa.org"-SSS official website) <https://images.search.yahoo.com/search/images?p=marshall+islands+people>

Above. Marshallese girls in hula skirt dance costume. (Photo credit: "pinterest.com" <<htttps://images.search.yahoo.com/search/images?p=marshall+islands+people>

After almost four decades under US administration as the easternmost part of the UN Trust Territory of the Pacific Islands, the Marshall Islands attained independence in 1986 under a Compact of Free Association. Compensation claims continue as a result of US nuclear testing on some of the atolls between 1947 and 1962. The Marshall Islands hosts the US Army Kwajalein Atoll Reagan Missile Test Site, a key installation in the US missile defense network. Kwajalein also hosts one of four dedicated ground antennas (the others are on Ascension (Saint Helena, Ascension, and Tristan da Cunha), Diego Garcia (British Indian Ocean Territory), and at Cape Canaveral, Florida (US)) that assist in the operation of the Global Positioning System (GPS) navigation system. *(World Factbook, op.cit.)*

Behind the unwary Marshallese children is the rising sea level – climate change. (Photo credit: "gberg.net" https://images.search.yahoo.com/search/images?p=marshall+islands+people+)

"Rising seas are claiming a vulnerable nation"

By Coral Davenport. Photographs and video by Josh Haner.

https://www.nytimes.com/interactive/2015/12/02/world/The-Marshall-Islands-Are-Disappearing.html

"EBEYE, Marshall Islands — Linber Anej waded out in low tide to haul concrete chunks and metal scraps to shore and rebuild the makeshift sea wall in front of his home. The temporary barrier is no match for the rising seas that regularly flood the shacks and muddy streets with saltwater and raw sewage, but every day except Sunday, Mr. Anej joins a group of men and boys to haul the flotsam back into place."

High waves strike Marshall Island houses at seashore – climate change (Photo credit: "www.nationalobserver.com" - https://images.search.yahoo.com/search/images?p=marshall+islands+people+)

> "Worlds away, in plush hotel conference rooms in Paris, London, New York and Washington, Tony A. deBrum, the foreign minister of the Marshall Islands, tells the stories of men like Mr. Anej to convey to more powerful policy makers the peril facing his island nation in the Pacific as sea levels rise — and to shape the legal and financial terms of a major United Nations climate change accord now being negotiated in Paris."

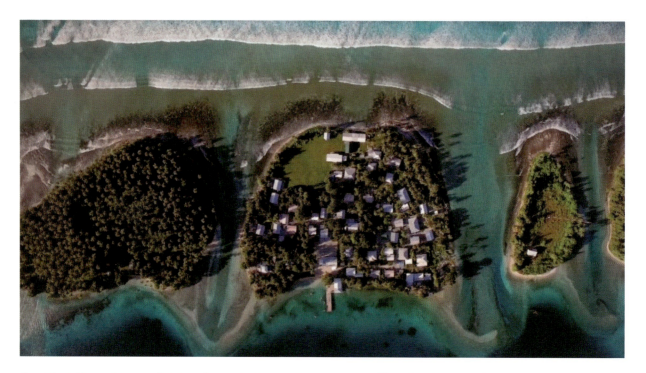

Small atolls in Marshall Islands are being submerged by climate change. (Photo credit: www.paralanaturaleza.org <
<https://images.search.yahoo.com/search/images?p=marshall+islands>

"Mr. deBrum's focus is squarely on the West's wallets — recouping "loss and damage," in negotiators' parlance, for the destruction wrought by the rich nations' industrial might on the global environment. Many other low-lying nations are just as threatened by rising seas. In Bangladesh, some 17 percent of the land could be inundated by 2050, displacing about 18 million people. But the Marshall Islands holds an important card: Under a 1986 compact, the roughly 70,000 residents of the Marshalls, because of their long military ties to Washington, are free to emigrate to the United States, a pass that will become more enticing as the water rises on the islands' shores."

Majuro airport. (Photo credit: www.tourist-destinations.com-

"For Mr. deBrum, a warming planet is not abstract. As the burning of fossil fuels increases heat-trapping gases in the atmosphere, the planet warms, and the Greenland and Antarctic ice sheets melt into the oceans. Sea levels are projected to rise one to four feet across the globe by the end of the century, a series of major international scientific reports have concluded."

Majuro floods from climate change. (Photo credit: "thegreentimes.co.za" < <https://images.search.yahoo.com/search/images?p=marshall+islands>

"Most of the 1,000 or so Marshall Islands, spread out over 29 narrow coral atolls in the South Pacific, are less than six feet above sea level — and few are more than a mile wide. For the Marshallese, the destructive power of the rising seas is already an inescapable part of daily life. Changing global trade winds have raised sea levels in the South Pacific about a foot over the past 30 years, faster than elsewhere. Scientists are studying whether those changing trade winds have anything to do with climate change."

Marshallese Ladies with welcome leis. (Photo credit: www.sharkdefenders.com) <https://images.search.yahoo.com/search/images?p=marshall+islands+people+>

"In neighborhoods like Mr. Anej's, after the sewage-filled tides wash into homes, fever and dysentery soon follow. On other islands, the wash of saltwater has penetrated and salinated underground freshwater supply. On Majuro, flooding tides damaged hundreds of homes in 2013. The elementary school closed for nearly two weeks to shelter families. That same year, the airport temporarily closed after tides flooded the runway."

Rising sea level due to climate change has caused saltwater intrusion into the soil, that is destroying breadfruit and other agricultural crops. – EIA. (Photo credit: www.lapresse.ca - <https://images.search.yahoo.com/search/images?p=marshall+islands+people+images&fr>

> "The deal offered: an open door to the Marshallese and Bikini Islanders. That bargain has already fostered communities of thousands of Marshall Islanders in Springdale, Ark., and Salem, Ore., fleeing a deluged future. That 1986 compact also established a United States government fund to support Bikini Islanders — as long as they continued to live in the Marshall Islands. Now the Bikini Islanders want to use that fund to move to the United States."

Micronesia

People first settled Micronesia about 3,500 to 2,000 years ago. Language rather than archaeology has provided the most insight into the history of early settlement. The languages of eastern and central Micronesia are closely related to Austronesian languages that exist to the southeast in Melanesia. These islands on the western edge of Micronesia seem to have been settled from the Philippines and Indonesia.

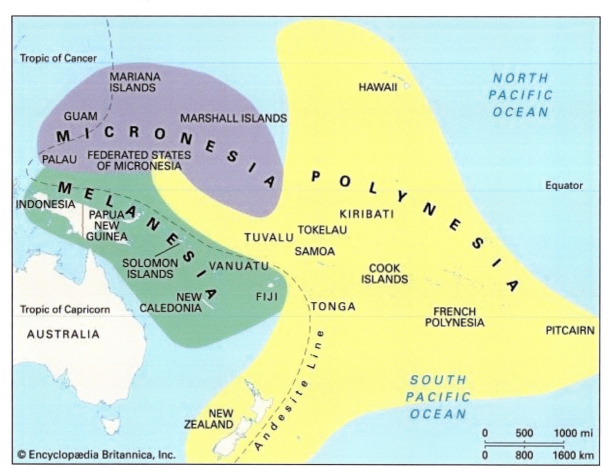

Micronesia, Polynesia, Melanesia culture areas. (Map from Encyclopedia Britannica Online. - https://www.britannica.com/place/Micronesia-cultural-region...)

The languages of Palau, Yap, and the Marianas are relatively distinct from each other and from other Micronesian languages, although they are clearly Austronesian in their general affiliation. The Chamorro language, spoken in the Marianas, has undergone much influence from Spanish and probably also from the Philippine Tagalog language after more than four centuries of Western contact.

"Sailing the Pacific"

Micronesian navigators have played an important role in the revival of Polynesian navigation. Mau Piailug (born 1932), who grew up on Satawal in the Federated States of Micronesia, where traditional navigation is still practiced, navigated the reconstructed Polynesian voyaging canoe *Hokule'a* on her maiden voyage from Hawaii to Tahiti in 1976. He later trained the Hawaiian navigator Nainoa Thompson, who subsequently trained many others. Voyaging continued into the 21st century, and in 2007 the *Hokule'a* sailed to Satawal to accompany the canoe *Alingano Maisu*, which was given as a gift to Mau Piailug to thank him for his contributions to the reawakening of Pacific voyaging traditions.

Outrigger canoe. Islanders of Satawal Island, Federated States of Micronesia, sail a hand-hewn outrigger canoe. The Satawal islanders are considered the best sea explorers of the wide Austronesian Pacific islands. (Photo credit - © Nicholas DeVore III/Bruce Coleman Inc. – https://www.britannica.com/place/Micronesia-cultural-region...)

A typical Micronesian community had one or more meetinghouses. These served as social gathering places and as places to plan community affairs. The number and elaborateness of the meetinghouses were greatest in Palau and Yap. In Palau, Yap, and the western atolls, meetinghouses were used mostly by men, while farther east, women and children also entered them freely much of the time. Canoe houses were another important form of building throughout Micronesia. Those big enough to store the larger canoes were on the scale of meetinghouses and often were used as such in some areas. Small buildings for the isolation of menstruating women were common in the western Carolines, and they continued to be used in Yap until well into the 20th century.

"Bai" - A traditional bai, or meetinghouse; at the Belau National Museum, Koror, Palau.

(Photo credit - Matt Kieffer – https://www.britannica.com/place/Micronesia-cultural-region...)

Nauru

Nauru, a country in Oceania, is officially called the Republic of Nauru and formerly known as Pleasant Island. It is an island country in Micronesia in the Central Pacific. Its nearest neighbour is Banaba Island in Kiribati, 300 kilometres to the east. (*Data source*: <https://en.wikipedia.org/wiki/Nauru>)

It lies just south of the equator and west of Kiribati. Inhabited by a population of mainly Polynesian ancestry, Nauru was explored by the British in 1798 and became a German protectorate in 1888. Nauru was administered by Australia from 1914 until it became independent in 1968. The capital is Yaren; population: 13,500.

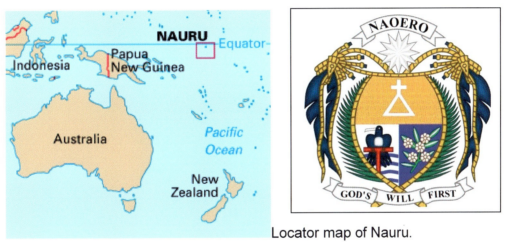

Locator map of Nauru.
"geography.howstuffworks.com/oceania-and-australia/geography-of..."

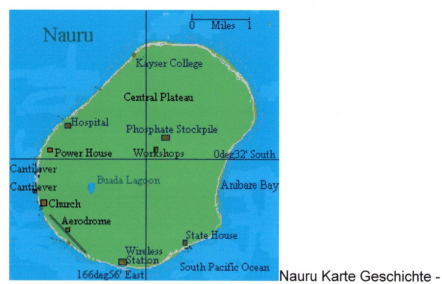Nauru Karte Geschichte - www.lahistoriaconmapas.com/atlas/landkarte/Nauru-Karte-Geschichte.htm"

Nauru hula dancers. (Left group photo: "tropicalcyclocross.com/cgi/people-of-nauru"). Right solo photo: Nauru girl - www.janeresture.com/nauru. < https://searchprivacy.co/?q=nauru history people>

Angam Day - The Government of the Republic of Nauru. (Photo credit: 'www.naurugov.nr/about-nauru/nauruans") <https://searchprivacy.co/?q=nauru history people>

New Caledonia

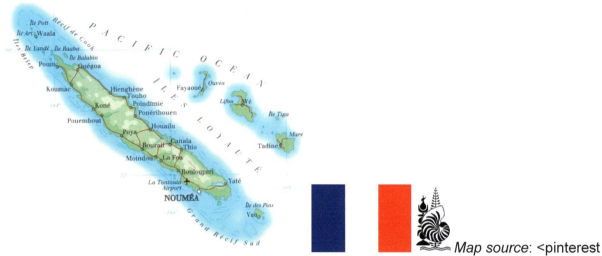

Map source: <pinterest < https://www.google.com/search?q=noumea> *Flag & Seal source:*
[http://en.wikipedia.org/wiki/Image:NC_Armoires.gif source and rights]- online Free Public Use.

Left - School Boys Singing, Island of Mare, New Caledonia: Baba ... (Photo credit - "dpreview.com/galleries/8193030067/photos/2339088/school-boys..."). Left - *Flag of the Independence Movements.*" Front de Libération Nationale Kanak Socialiste (FLNKS)" – Data source: http://www.newworldencyclopedia.org/entry/New_Caledonia

The western Pacific was first populated about 50,000 years ago. The Austronesians moved into the area later. The diverse group of people that settled over the Melanesian archipelagos are known as the Lapita. They arrived in the archipelago now commonly known as New Caledonia and the Loyalty Islands around 1500 B.C.E. The Lapita were highly skilled navigators and agriculturists with influence over a large area of the Pacific. From about the eleventh century,

Polynesians also arrived and mixed with the populations of the archipelago.

Nouméa (see photo above) is the capital of the South Pacific archipelago and overseas French territory New Caledonia. Situated on the main island, Grand Terre, it's known for beaches and its blend of French and native Kanak influences. The Jean-Marie Tjibaou Cultural Centre showcases Kanak heritage, and the Musée de Nouvelle-Calédonie has exhibits from across the Pacific region. The Aquarium des Lagons introduces local marine life. *(Data source: <https://www.google.com/destination?q=new+caledonia>)*

Social and racial discrimination practiced by whites commingled all Pacific blacks, and then only those from New Caledonia, under the term "Kanak." The name "Kanaky" is favored by Melanesian nationalists. The word comes from "kanaka," a Polynesian word meaning "human." The French later used the word to describe all the native inhabitants of the South Pacific Ocean. The word, turned into "Canaque" in French, became derogative. When Melanesian inhabitants started to form political parties, this derogative word became a symbol of political emancipation and pride.

Kanak conical house. Note the door posts. (Photo credit: by Fanny Schertzer - self-made, CC BY-SA 3.0, https://commons.wikimedia.org/w/index.php?curid=3520983)

The indigenous Melanesian Kanak community represented 44.6 percent of the population at the 1996 census, a proportion that has declined due to immigration. Kanaks consider themselves the black people of the Western Pacific, with links to Papuans and Australian Aborigines, and call themselves *Ti-Va-Ouere*, or "Brothers of the Earth."

Kanak women in New Caledonia. (Photo source:. Bananaflo. Own work assumed (based on copyright claims)., CC BY-SA 3.0, https://commons.wikimedia.org/w/index.php?curid=681195

The rest of the population is made up of ethnic groups that arrived in the past 150 years. Europeans make up 34.5 percent (the majority are French with German, British, and Italian minorities), Polynesians (Wallisians and Tahitians), 11.8 percent; Indonesians, 2.6 percent; Vietnamese, 1.4 percent; Ni-Vanuatu, 1.2 percent; and various other groups. *(Data source: http://www.newworldencyclopedia.org/entry/New_Caledonia)*

New Caledonia dance group. (Photo source: <www.ireneviaggi.it/2012_site/viaggi-di-nozze/programmaviaggio-41...>

New Caledonia: The Kanak People & Tjibaoou Cultural Centre. Left - Statue wood carving; right – doorpost. (Photo credit: ...<https://www.flickr.com/photos/tanweecheng/4737542747) - Jean-Marie Tjibaou Cultural Centre, Nouméa.

New Caledonia, or *Nouvelle-Calédonie*, is an overseas territory of France. British explorer James Cook named the territory's main island "New Caledonia" because the island's purple hills reminded him of the the Scottish Highlands. New Caledonia's capital, Nouméa, is the seat of the Secretariat of the Pacific Community, formed by Australia, France, the Netherlands, New Zealand, the United Kingdom, and the United States in 1947 to promote economic and social stability in the countries of the South Pacific.

Population (2011 estimates) 256,275; 209 census 245,580.

New Zealand (Maori) - (www.unflags.com)

(Photo credit: Shutterstock)

Coat of Arms, NZ, from Heraldry of the World, Online.

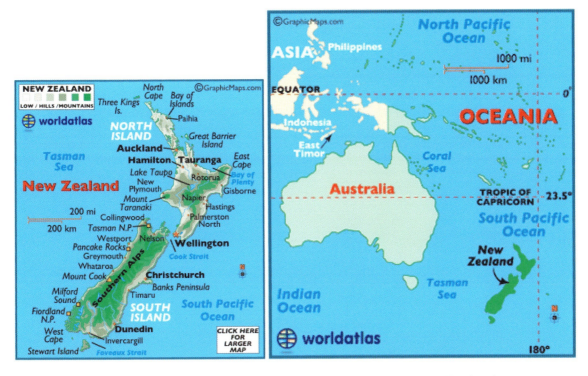

Map Source. <file:///C:/Users/Noel/Documents/Austronesia/New%20Zealand-Maori/New%20Zealand%20Map%20-%20Map%20of%20New%20Zealand,%20New%20Zealand%20Outline%20Map%20-%20World%20Atlas.html>Free Stock Images - For Personal & Commercial Use | dreamstime.comwww.dreamstime.com/Stock_Images/Chosen_Photos

The first inhabitants of Aotearoa – the most widely known Maori name for New Zealand, means "the land of the long white cloud." Their ancestors were the East Polynesian people. There are

Moana, the Disney animated film was inspired by Austronesian characters. Most especially, the body tattoo of the leading man was drawn from the Maori.

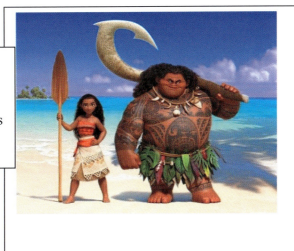

number of theories about the origins of the
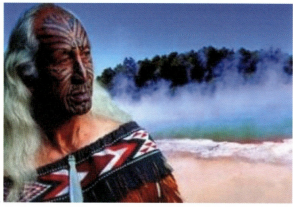
Maori.

Maori legends say that they came from "Hawaiki" about 1000 years ago. The word "Hawaiki" features in the mythology as the homeland of the Maori, before they traveled across the sea to New Zealand. The most popular mass migration theory is called "The Great Fleet". In 1350 these group of Polynesians took a fleet of several canoes to get to New Zealand and according to legend, this fleet arrived from the mythical home of Hawaiki. Some believe that the first settlers found Aotearoa probably by chance or mistake as they could have been blown off course in one of their navigation. Most of historians affirm that Maori ancestors migrated from China, travelled via Taiwan, the Philippines to Indonesia, onto Melanesia, reaching Fiji, from there to Samoa and on to the Marquesas, then turned South West to Tahiti, then to the Cook Island and finally to New Zealand. *(Data source: www.themaori.com)*

In the past decade and a half, geneticists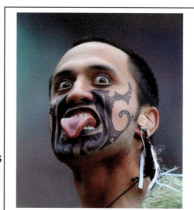

have confirmed what linguists and archaeologists had been saying since the 1970s - that there is a clear lineage running from Taiwan's inhabitants of 5000 years ago to modern-day

Polynesians, including Maori.

Maori and indigenous Taiwanese are cousins.

Victoria University biologist Dr Geoff Chambers, an expert on the Maori-Taiwanese connection. It all started, said Chambers, about 5000 years ago when a group of people, now known as Austronesians, began to make forays south from their home in Taiwan, spreading first to the nearby Batenes Islands, then to the Philippines and beyond.

About 3000 years ago, in what is now Papua New Guinea, the Austronesians encountered another major group, the Papuans, who are closely related to modern-day Australian Aboriginals. Intermarriage between the groups, in a genetic mix of about 70 per cent

Austronesian and 30 per cent Papuan, produced the ancestors of the modern Polynesians.

The proto-Polynesians, with their unique genetic mix, then "sailed into the Pacific, settled it, and arrived in New Zealand about 750 years ago", says Chambers.

Back in Asia, other Austronesians kept moving and mixing. Today, 350 million people have some Austronesian heritage, and they're spread from Madagascar off the African coast to Easter Island near South America, though the biggest groups are in Indonesia and the Philippines.

Some Austronesians, though, stayed put in Taiwan for five millennia, experiencing little genetic intermingling. The upshot, says Chambers, is that "there's a very real sense in which the

aboriginal people of Taiwan are the living ancestors of Maori".

Over the millennia, Taiwan's stay-at-home Austronesians have divided into distinct tribes with clearly differentiated languages, physical appearance and cultural practices. All are related to Polynesians, but there are "tantalising" clues to suggest the east coast's Amis people are most

closely related.

The first 10 counting numbers in Maori and Amis are: tahi=cecay; rua=toso; toro=tolo; wha=sepat; rima=lima; ono=enem; whitu=pito; waru=falo; iwa=siwa; tekau=polo. *(Text source: Adam Dudding, NZ. Last updated 17:45, March 15 2015. www.stuff.co.nz/travel/destinations/asia/67390585/New-Zealands-long-lost-Taiwanese-cuzziesNiue)*

<u>Note the similarities</u>: The Bahasa Indonesia counting is: "2=dua"; "4=empat"; "5=lima"; "6=enam"; "7=tujuh"; "8=wolo"; "10=sepuluh". In Philippine Tagalog: "2=dalawa"; "3=tatlo"; "4=apat"; "5=lima"; "6=anim"; "7=pito"; "8=walo"; "10=sampu". In Phil-Bisaya, "2=duha".

Palau

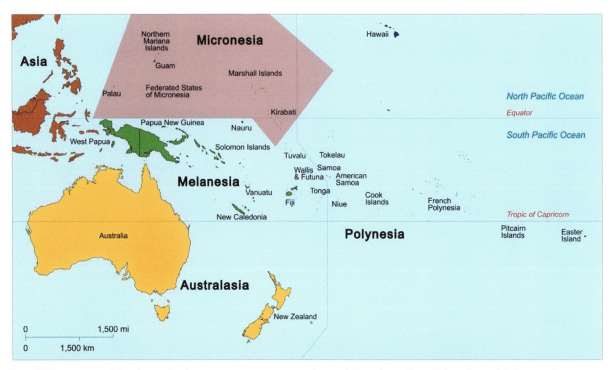

The Palauan archipelago is the westernmost portion of the Caroline Islands, which are in turn part of the Micronesian geographical subdivision of Oceania. East of Mindanao in the Philippines, Palau is 722 nautical miles (1,340 kilometers) southwest of Guam. Palau's three hundred volcanic and raised coral islands and atolls rise up from the Philippine Plate, with the highest stone outcrops reaching about 720 feet (2,220 meters) on the largest island, Babel thuap. The islands have a total land area of 191 square miles (495 square kilometers). The weather is hot and humid, with annual rainfall around 150 inches (3,800 milimeters). The flora and fauna are tropical, but Palau is best known for its 70-mile-long (113-kilometer-long) barrier reef which encloses spectacular coral reefs and a lagoon of approximately 560 square miles (1,450 square kilometers), a divers' paradise. The capital is Koror, which in 1004 was to be relocated to Melekeok in Babaelthuap. (Read more: *http//www.everyculture.om/No-Sa/Palau.html#ixzz50alXBSPW*).

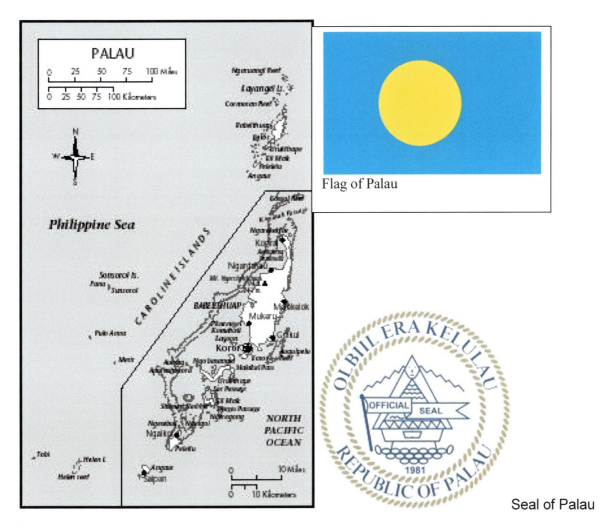

Flag of Palau

Seal of Palau

Politically Micronesia encompasses, together with Guam, the Commonwealth of the Northern Mariana Islands, the Republic of the Marshall Islands, the Federated States of Micronesia and Palau.

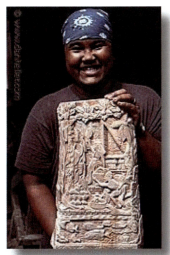

Palau woodcarver – storyboard. (Photo credit: Dan Heller http://www.danheller.com/palau-misc.html)

According to current evidence, the peopling of Micronesia took place over several thousands of years. The first colonizing event occurred in the Mariana Islands about 3,500 years ago, from a source in Island Southeast Asia. The second event was slightly later, about 3,000 years ago in Palau, from a different source in Island Southeast Asia. The third was in Yap, evident by 2,000 years ago but perhaps earlier, coming probably from Island Melanesia. The fourth was also about 2,000 years ago and continuing over 100-200 years throughout most of central and eastern Micronesia, and these populations came probably came from Island Melanesia or perhaps parts of Indonesia. The fifth migration settlement in Micronesia was an unusual case within the last 1,000 years, when Indonesian communities moved from east to west and settled in the few remaining uninhabited or under-utilized spaces of Micronesia. *(Data source: Austronesian Migrations and Developments in Micronesia, Mike T. Carson, Research Associate, Micronesian Area Research Center, University of Guam/mtcarson@uguam.uog.edu*

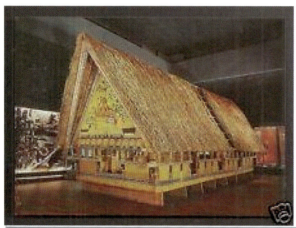

Traditional Palau "Bai" or "house". Note the gable which is regarded as an important part of the bai. (Photo credit: http://www.everyculture.com/No-Sa/Palau.html)

Linguistic Affiliation. Palauan is considered an Austronesian language of a Western subgroup, *Palau,* which along with Chamorro (Mariana Islands) is considered separate from the other Micronesian and Pacific languages grouped under the label "Oceanic."
(Read more: http://www.everyculture.com/No-Sa/Palau.html#ixzz50ZuUXCnj)

http://www.everyculture.com/No-Sa/Palau.html

Yap Island Hula Dancers. Photo Credit: Brad Holland, https://palaudiveadventures.com/diving-micronesia/#

Papua New Guinea (Outer Islands)

(Above) - PNG Flag - By User:Nightstallion - Own work, FOTW, Public Domain, https://commons.wikimedia.org/w/index.php?curid=433185

(Right)-PNG Seal - By SodacanThis vector image was created with Inkscape. - Own work, CC BY-SA 4.0, https://commons.wikimedia.org/w/index.php?curid=61071416

Map of Papua New Guinea. The Austronesians settled in the "outer islands" and are called "Melanesians", brown skin. The mainland is predominantly of African ancestry, black skin and kinky hair.

"Hiri Motu" annual festival. Melanesians of the Outer Islands, Papua New Guinea – celebrating the bringing of sago from the mainland to the Outer Islands in exchange from pots and clay jars made by Melanesians and carried on boats. (Photo Credit: Juan Miguel, NZ, FB, Oct 2107, Free Public Use Online)

Melanesian grass skirt dancer performing during the "Hiri Motu" Festival, Papua New Guinea, 2016. *(Photo credit: Juan mIguel, NZ, FB, Free Public Use Online).*

Melanesian band from Papua New Guinea (Outer Islands) performing in the 2016 Pasifika Festival in New Zealand. (Photo credit: Joey Miguel, FB, Oct 2017, Free Online Public Use).

Melanesians of mixed ancestry during the Pasifika Festival, New Zealand, 2016. (Photo credit: Juan Miguel, NZ, FB, Oct 2017)

Melanesians of African ancestry from the mainland of Papua New Guinea making sago. (Photo credit: Juan Miguel, New Zealand, FB, Free Public Use Online).

Melanesian children, Papua New Guinea. (Photo credit: Dreamstime.com)

Melanesian bamboo house, Papua New Guinea. (Photo credit: PNG Ministry of Tourism, Free Online Public Use from the Internet). Editor's note: This type of palm-roofed house built of bamboo is common throughout the Austronesian islands of the Pacific, including the Philippines, Indonesia, Malaysia, Thailand, etc.

Philippines

Philippine Austronesians

Baguio Igorot Ceremony, Mt. Province, Philippines. (Photo credit – downloaded from the Internet, Free Public Use)

Gong Festival, Mt. Province, Philippines. (Photo credit – downloaded from the Internet, Free Public Online Use)

The Philippine coconut drink is common throughout the Pacific island Austronesian groups. (Photo credit: Marissa Torres Langseth, HAPI (Humanist Alliance Philippines International, Nov 2017, FB).

Annual Masskara Festival, Bacolod, Negros, Philippines – usually held 3rd week of October. (Photo credit – Marissa Torres Langseth, HAPI - Humanist Alliance Philippines International, Bacolod General Assembly, 2018 brochure)  *Filipina beauties, Bailen, Cavite, Philippines.* (Photo credit: Cesar Pareja, Bailen, Cavite, Philippines, FB, Nov 2017).

Two young Filipina Austronesians – Bela (5 years old) and Bea (4 years old), sisters - preparing for a hula dance, Makati, Metro Manila, Philippines, October 2017. Continuing the Austronesian grass skirt tradition of the Pacific Islands. (Photo Credit: E. I. Astillero. Note – they are my granddaughters from my 2nd daughter, Iriz Anjelica. Photo taken with my Zenfone.)

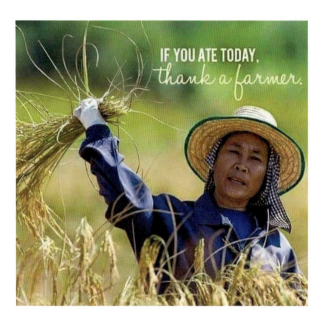

Filipino Austronesian farmer. (Pic credit – downloaded from the Internet, Free Public Use Online)

Most rural farms using wet paddies still use the Philippine "carabao" – "kerbau" in Bahasa Indonesia, indicating close affinity in languages within the Austronesian family. (Photo credit – Marissa Torres Langseth, HAPI Page-FB, Nov 2017)

Above. Filipina police officers´ parade using Austronesian-design skirts from Northern Philippines. (Pic credit – Tiz Wezza, FB)

"Young woman rules Mandaya land"

By: Frinston Lim - @inquirerdotnet Philippine Daily Inquirer / 05:54 AM November 12, 201 – posted in FB.

Above. Amid a heavy downpour, students in their traditional Mandaya (Davao Province, Philippines) attire continue performing during the Kalindugan Festival. (Photos By Eden Jhan Licayan)

CARAGA, DAVAO ORIENTAL — Christine Banugan, 26, takes her role seriously as the new "likid," or chieftain, of a cluster of Mandaya communities of mostly aging people in the upland village of Pichon in this town.

Below. A new female chieftain is blessed in a Mandaya Austronesian group, Davao, Philippines, November 2017.

The new Mandaya lady-chieftain (sitting left) is a modern college-educated bank executive from Davao City. She will lead the mountain tribe in their programs for social services, land rights, and economic opportunities.

Filipino Austronesians with their fighting cocks. (Photo credit: FB, Free Public Use Online, Nov 2017). Editor's note: cockfighting is found in almost all Austronesian Pacific island groups, and in Southeast Asia.

Left. A roasted pig. A favourite, traditional Austronesian delicacy served for special occasions - widespread across Austronesian countries – except, perhaps, in Islamic groups. This one is in the Philippines. (Photo credit – downloaded from the Internet, Free Public Use Online)

Above. An over-loaded Philippine jeepney. (Photo Credit: Urban Rural Consulting Services, FB, Nov 2017)

Filipino children in a nutrition feeding program by HAPI – Humanist Alliance Philippines International. (Photo credit: Jamie del Rosario-Martinez, HAPI Project Coordinator, Barangay Ilaya, Muntinlupa, Metro Manila, Philippines, Nov 2017).

Samoa

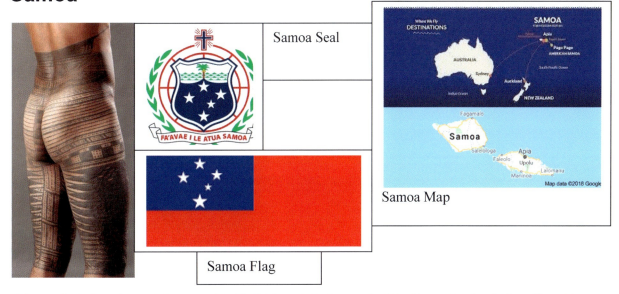

(Above, left) Traditional Samoan body tattoo. (Photo credit: FB, Free Public Online Use, Nov 2017)

Samoa is a country comprising the westernmost group of the Samoan Islands, in Polynesia. Many of its islands have reef-bordered beaches and rugged, rainforested interiors with gorges and waterfalls. The islands include Upolu, home to most of Samoa's population, and Savai'i, one of the largest islands in the South Pacific. Smaller islands may have small villages or be uninhabited, some with wildlife sanctuaries. Capital: Apia. Currency: Samoan tālā. Official languages: English, Samoan. (Data source: *https://en.wikipedia.org/wiki/Samoa*)

The Independent State of Samoa (Samoan: *Malo Sa'oloto Tuto'atasi o Sāmoa*), commonly known as Samoa - Samoan: *Sāmoa*, and, until 1997, known as Western Samoa, is a unitary parliamentary democracy with eleven administrative divisions. The two main islands are Savai'i and Upolu with four smaller islands surrounding the landmasses. The capital city is Apia. The Lapita people discovered and settled the Samoan Islands around 3,500 years ago. They developed a unique Samoan language and Samoan cultural identity.

Samoa is a member of the Commonwealth of Nations. Western Samoa was admitted to the United Nations on 15 December 1976. The entire island group, which includes American Samoa, was called "Navigator Islands" by European explorers before the 20th century because of the Samoans' seafaring skills. (Data source: *https://en.wikipedia.org/wiki/Samoa*)

Photo credit: Pixabay; dxnews)

(Photo credit: pacificrisa.org; skyscanner)

Samoa family infront of open-walled house – (Photo credit: Global Education)

Samoa Flag Day, Carson City, California, USA, 1ST Week August 2017 – (Photo credit: Federation of Samoans)

For years, it was generally accepted that Polynesians originated in modern-day Taiwan and began moving south and east about 4,000 years ago. This migration account is based on the research of linguists, the findings of archeologists and some genetic analysis.(Google Search- Feb 7, 2011)

Related ethnic groups. Māori, Fijians, other Polynesian peoples, Malays, Filipinos and other Austronesian People. The Samoan people are a Polynesian ethnic group of the Samoan Islands, sharing genetics, language, history and culture.
(https://www.google.com/search?q=samoa+origins...)

Solomon Islands

The Solomon Islands were initially settled by at least 2000 bce—well before the archaeological record begins—probably by people of the Austronesian language group. Pottery of the Lapita culture was in use in Santa Cruz and the Reef Islands about 1500 bce. Material dating to about 1000 bce has also been excavated at Vatuluma Cave (Guadalcanal), on Santa Ana Island, and on the outlying islands of Anuta and Tikopia. *(Encyclopedia Britannica Online Free Public Use)*

Above, schoolchildren, Solomon Islands. (Photo credit: Living Ocean Foundation)

The first European to reach the islands was the Spanish explorer Álvaro de Mendaña de Neira in 1568. Subsequently, unjustified rumours led to the belief that he had not only found gold there but had also discovered where the biblical king Solomon obtained the gold for his temple in

Jerusalem. The islands thus acquired the name Islas de Solomón. Later Spanish expeditions to the southwest Pacific in 1595 and 1606 were unable to confirm the discoveries reported by Mendaña.

Marau women, Solomon Islands. (Photo credit: W-T-W.org)

About 4,000 years ago, Austronesian peoples moved into the area, arriving by sea from Southeast Asia. By 3,500 years ago they had occupied parts of the islands of the Bismarck Archipelago. Their presence is marked by the appearance of the distinctive pottery, tools, and shell ornaments that define the "Lapita culture". They spoke an Austronesian language related to languages of the Philippines and Indonesia and ancestral to many of the languages of coastal eastern New Guinea; much of the Bismarck Archipelago; the Solomons, Vanuatu, and New Caledonia; and those of central and eastern Micronesia and Polynesia. *(Data source: https://www.britannica.com/place/Melanesia)*

 (Left) Lapita pottery design scattered throughout Austronesian Pacific islands and indicating a commonality of culture.

Evidence of long-distance trade, particularly of shell ornaments and obsidian, suggests that the widely spread communities characterized by the Lapita tradition had become linked politically by 3,000–3,500 years ago. The settlement of eastern Micronesia by Austronesian speakers, perhaps from the Solomons, apparently took place during this period. Fiji was initially colonized by Lapita peoples and became a springboard to the settlement of western Polynesia.

Below, right, Snooker Hut Girl, Solomon Islands. (Photo credit: 7th Day Adventists)

Above. Grass skirt dancers welcome visitors with traditional Austronesian songs and dances. (Photo credit: Iheringer Worldpress,com)

Solomon Islands boat crew. (Photo credit: www.visitsolomons.com.sb)

Thailand

Thai Austronesians

The Austro-Tai peoples consist of both the Austronesian and Tai peoples. Today, the Daic (Tai) peoples live in southern China (Yunnan, Guangxi, Guizhou, Hainan, Guangdong), the Southeast Asian mainland countries of Thailand, Laos, Myanmar, and Vietnam, as well as parts of northeastern India. The Austronesian peoples can be found in the Philippines, Malaysia, Vietnam, Indonesia, Madagascar, Oceania, and various other locations throughout the Pacific Rim.

The table below lists 20 Thai words with their respective transliterations and Austronesian cognates that have not deviated from Proto-Austronesian. Proto-Malayo-Polynesian forms reconstructed by Robert Blust are also given. The Austronesian languages are given by Tagalog, Ilocano, and Malay, all of which are major lingua francas in Southeast Asia today. The words given below can also be found in Swadesh lists.

Note: For Proto-Malayo-Polynesian, "q" is a glottal stop, not a "k" sound.

English	Thai ภาษาไทย	Thai transliteration	Austronesian language	Proto-Malayo-Polynesian[9]
I	กู	kuu	ko (Tagalog)	*ku
you	มึง	mɯŋ	mo (Tagalog)	*mu
bird	นก	nók	manok (Tagalog)	*manuk
eye	ตา	taa	mata (Tagalog)	*mata

---

[9] http://language.psy.auckland.ac.nz/austronesian/language.php?id=269 – Blust, Robert (1999)

tooth	ฟัน	fan	ngipin (Tagalog)	*ipen
tongue	ลิ้น	lín	dila (Tagalog), lidah (Malay)	*dilaq
hand	มือ	mɯɯ	ima (Ilocano), kamay (Tagalog)	*[qa]lima
leg	ขา	khăa	kaki (Malay)	*qaqay
liver	ตับ	tàp	atay (Tagalog)	*qatay
moon	เดือน	dɯan	bulan (Ilocano and Malay)	*bulan
water	น้ำ	náam	danum (Ilocano)	*danum
rain	ฝน	fŏn	hujan (Malay), ulan (Tagalog)	*quzan
fire	ไฟ	fay	apoy (Tagalog)	*hapuy
road	ทาง	thaaŋ	daan (Tagalog)	*zalan
black	ดำ	dam	hitam (Malay), itim (Tagalog)	*ma-qitem
to drink	ดื่ม	dɯɯm	inom (Tagalog)	*inum
to eat	กิน	kin	kain (Tagalog)	*kaen
to bite	กัด	kàt	kagat (Tagalog)	*kaʀat
to die	ตาย	taay	matay (Tagalog)	*m-atay
this	นี้	níi	ini (Malay)	*i ni

The Thai Austronesians dwell in the nountainous areas of Thailand, and maintain their culture. The lowland Thais are mostly Buddhists. (Photo credit – downloaded from the Internet, Free Public Online Use)

Thai (Daic) – Austronesians. (Photo credit: Wikipedia, Free Online Public Use)

Thai-Austronesian language family (Data source: onlychaam.com "Ethnic Groups in Thailand" <March 23 2016/Stephanie>)	
Malayo-Polynesian group	
Cham	Mostly in Cambodia (where half of their population was exterminated by the Khmer rouge) and Vietnam, only 4,000 in Thailand.

Malay	3 million in Thailand, mostly in the south.
Moken (Sea Gypsies)	3,000 in the Andaman Sea on the west coast of Thailand (Krabi, Phuket, Phang Nga, Ranong), well know for their knowledge of the sea.
Urak Lawoi	1,000 to 3,000 (sources vary) in Phuket, also refered to as "Sea Gypsies".

Tonga

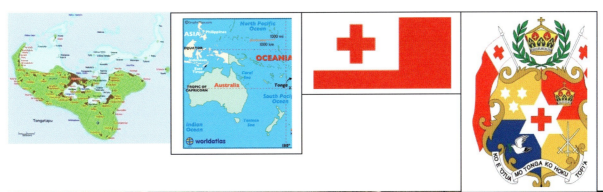

"Tonga Was Once The Heart of a Mighty Trading Empire in Prehistoric Oceania"

"A forgotten history. Tonga was once at the centre of a vast trading empire stretching 500,000 square kilometres (193,000 square miles) across the Pacific. (Chris Pash, *Business Insider*. 30 Sep 2017)"

"Stone tools imported during the last 1,000 years from Fiji, Samoa, and the Society Islands reveal that the maritime empire of Tonga served as a hub through which prehistoric people exchanged products and political ideas, according to a study."

"From about 1200 AD, the state of Tonga integrated the archipelago under a centralised authority and emerged as a unique maritime empire which engaged in long distance economic and political commerce."

"The stone tools found in Tonga came from Fiji, Samoa, and Tahiti, 2,500 km (1,553 miles) away."

Below are male dancers from Tonga at the 2015 Pasifik Festival in New Zealand. (Photo credit – downloaded from the Internet, Online Free Public Use)

Tuvalu

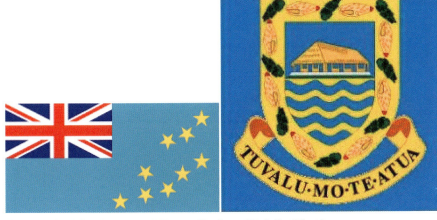

(Data Source: Tuvalu Travel Guide, Internet Free Online Public Use)

Tuvalu is a Polynesian island nation located in the Pacific Ocean, about midway between Hawaii and Australia, lying east-northeast of the Santa Cruz Islands (belonging to the Solomons), southeast of Nauru, south of Kiribati, west of Tokelau, northwest of Samoa and Wallis and Futuna .

Tuvalu, in the South Pacific, is an independent island nation within the British Commonwealth. Its 9 islands comprise small, thinly populated atolls and reef islands with palm-fringed beaches and WWII sites. Off Funafuti, the capital, the Funafuti Conservation Area offers calm waters for diving and snorkelling among sea turtles and tropical fish, plus several uninhabited islets sheltering sea birds. Population: 11,097 (2016) World Bank

Funafuti

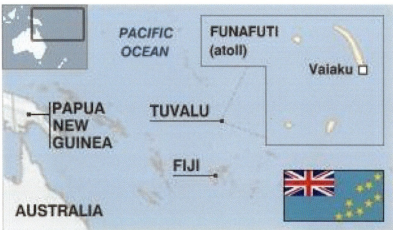

Tuvalu is a group of nine tiny islands in the South Pacific which won independence from the United Kingdom in 1978.

Formerly known as the Ellice Islands, all are low-lying, with no point on Tuvalu being higher than 4.5m above sea level. Local politicians have campaigned against climate change, arguing that it could see the islands swamped by rising sea levels.

Life on the islands is simple and often harsh. There are no streams or rivers, so the collection of rain is essential.

Coconut palms cover most of the islands, and copra - dried coconut kernel - is practically the only export commodity. Increasing salination of the soil threatens traditional subsistence farming. (Data Source: BBC News, Free Online Public Use)

Vanuatu

Vanuatu's name is derived from the word vanua ("land" or "home"), which occurs in several Austronesian languages, and the word tu ("stand"). Together the two words indicated the independent status of the new country. (https://en.wikipedia.org/wiki/Vanuatu)

"Origins of Vanuatu and Tonga's first people revealed" *(Data source: Tiz Wezza, FB, 4 October 2016)*

"The people of Vanuatu today are descended from Asia first of all. Their original base population is Asian. They came out of Taiwan and passing through the northern Philippines."

"The origins of Vanuatu and Tonga's first inhabitants has been revealed in a surprise discovery made by ANU(Australia National University) archaeologists in the first major study of ancient DNA (aDNA) from the Pacific Islands."

"The study, published in the scientific journal *Nature*, reveals Vanuatu's first people arrived 3,000 years ago from Taiwan and northern Philippines, and not from the neighbouring Australo-Papuan populations of Australia, New Guinea and the Solomon Islands that had been in the region for between 40,000 and 50,000 years."

"The people of Vanuatu today are descended from Asia first of all. Their original base population is Asian. They were straight out of Taiwan and perhaps the northern Philippines," said Professor Spriggs of the ANU School of Archaeology and Anthropology in the College of Arts and Social Sciences."

Nguna Island, Vanuatu. (Photo credit – gettyimages)

(Above) Live volcano, Vanuatu. (Right) "Dugong" – "Manatee". (Photo credit: islamoradatimes.com)

Viet Nam

Bamboo dance in rural Viet Nam. The Philippines has a bamboo dance - the "Tinikling" which mimics the white heron bird jumping over bamboo traps in the rice paddies. (Photo credit – Tizz Weza, FB)

Viet Namese hill tribes people laughing with lowland Viet Namese tourist, Note the Austronesian facial features and the weave design of the clothing. Check the design with Filipino hill tribes, Indonesian Flores groups, Thai-Daic Austronesian groups, and others. (Photo credit: VN Tourism Office)

Austronesian Viet Namese hill tribe children. (Photo credit: VN Government)

Part Three. Old Philippines

Overview

This section is a "pictorial".

A Chinese proverb says "a picture is worth a thousand words". I have selected old pictures of the Filipinos to illustrate that then, and now, the physiognomy or physical characteristics of the Filipino looks just like his blood cousins in Polynesia, Melanesia, Micronesia, and as far as Easter Island in the outermost eastern reaches of the Austronesian family.

"Balangay" – the Austronesian boat that carried migration from Taiwan to the Philippines, and thence, to the wide Pacific Ocean. (Photo credit - https://www.pinterest.com/pin/113223378110859699/)

 Gen. Gregorio del Pilar, 1896 – the Philippine's youngest revolutionary leader against Spain. (Photo credit: Old Philippines, Pinterest - online)

"Binukot" – two modern Filipinas dress up for this Austronesian dress design. (Photo credit: Maginoo Filipino, online – Philippine Indigenous Peoples)

Datuh Rajah Munda Mandi, with his wife, Zamboanga, 1890. (Photo credit: Old Philippines, online)

Yakan girl from Basilan Island, off Zamboanga, Mindanao. (Photo credit: Pinterest, Online.)

Young girls in tribal costumes, Mindanao. (Photo credit: Pinterest, Philippine Culture, Online.)

Modern dance troupe performing Mindanao Austronesian-inspired tribal dance. Note the costume weave design – check this out with the Taiwan aboriginal weave design – Indonesian (Flores), Champa (Cambodia), and Thai-Daic tribe. (Photo credit: Old Philippines, Pinterest)

 "Harana" or "serenade" acting out this old tradition of Filipino courtship, showing young men playing guitars downbstairs and singing to the 3 maidens at the second floor of a large Filipino nipa hut. (Photo credit: Pinterest – Old Philippines, online)

 Kalinga girl with body tattoo of Mountain Province, North, the Cordilleras, North Luzon. Note tattoo design similar to Maori body tattoo design. See p. 117 – New Zealand (Maori)(Photo credit – Pinterest, Old Philippines, online)

Kalinga man dressed up in ceremonial attire, 1900, Mountain Province, the Cordilleras, north Luzon. (Photo credit – Pinterest, Old hilippines, online)

Tinggian young woman, Mountain Province, the Cordilleras, north Luzon, 1911. (Photo credit: Pinterest, Old Philippines, Online.)

 Ifugao Dance. (Postcards from the Philippines, online.)

 Tribal dance of the Kalinga's. Note the weave design of the cloth – similar to Taiwan aborigines, and the body tattoo, similar to Maori (see p. 117 – New Zealand/Maori) and other Austronesian groups in the Pacific. (Photo credit: Pinterest, Philippine folk dances, Online.)

Tribal elder of Benguet, Mt. Province, the Cordilleras, north Luzon, 1920. (Photo credit: Pinterest, Old Philippine, Online.)

Rice terraces in the Mountain Province, northern Luzon. Note similar agricultural method in Indonesia, Viet Nam, Malaysia, Madagascar (Malagasy) and other Austronesian Pacific communities.(Photo credit: Pinterest, Online.)

Moro women of Jolo, Sulu, 1898. (Photo credit: Pinterest, Old Philippines, online.)

Moro leaders, datus, 1900. (Photo credit: Pinterest, Old Philippines, online.)

Singkil, a traditional Moro dance of royalty. (Photo credit: Pinterest, Philippine folk dances, Online.)

Row of nipa huts, Paranaque, 1920. (Photo credit: Pinterest, Old Philippines, online.)

Coconut cooking oil peddlers, Manila, 1898. (Photo credit: Pinterest, Old Philippines, Online.)

Flower vendors infront of Binondo church, Manila, 1900. (Photo credit: Pinterest, Old Philippnes, Online.)

Sari-sari store, early 20th century. (Photo credit: Pinterest, Old Philippines, Online.)

Women of Pampanga, Central Luzon, 1820. (Photo credit: Pinterest, Old Philippines, Online.)

Lea, a Tagalog Filipina from Cavite, 1926. (Photo credit: Pinterest, Old Philippines, Online.)

Filipina weaver at her loom, Cavite, 1900. (Photo credit: Pinterest, Old Philippines, Online.)

Cuenco Family, 1900, Cebu, Old families in Colon Street, by Cecilia Brainhard, Blogger.

Two Filipina women after attending a catholic mass, Paco Manila, 1900. (Photo credit: Pinterest, Old Philippines, Online,)

American soldiers during the Philippine-American War, 1898-1904, (Photo credit: Pinterest, Old Philippines, Online.)

Two Filipinas from Taguig, Province of Rizal, 1898. (Photo credit: Pinterest, Old Philippines, Online.)

Young Filipina woman from Pandacan, Manila, 1899. (Photo credit: Pinterest, Old Philippines, Online.)

Young girls on the bamboo staircase of their nipa hut, 1900. (Photo credit: Pinterest, Old Philippines, Online.)

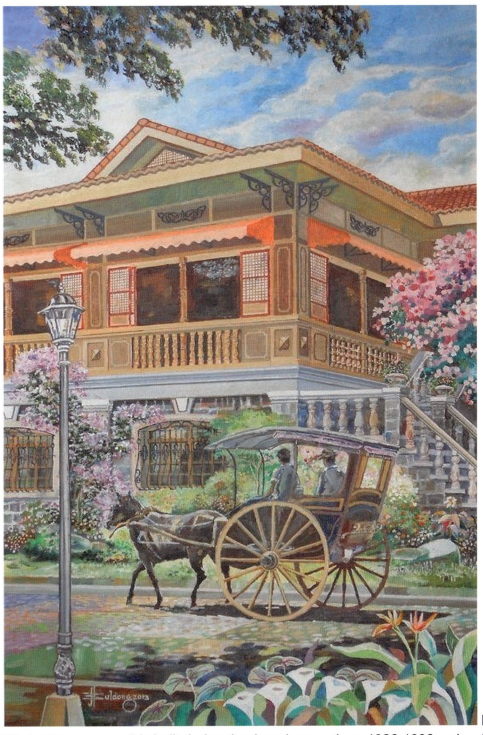

Painting of a large Filipino house, possibly built during the American regime, 1920-1930s, showing a calesa or "carromata" – horse-drawn hansom. (Photo credit: Pinterest, Philippine paintings, onine.)

 A festive rural village event – moving a house, painting by Fernando Amorsolo. (Photo credit: Philippine paintings, Pinterest, Online.)

 The sewing of the original Filipino flag by the Agoncillo sisters. This was the flag was raised, for the first time, on June 12, 1896 infront of the house of Gen. Emilio Aguinaldo, first Philippines president of the Republic, in Kawit, Kabite, where the Philippine Independence from Spain was officially declared while the armed revolution was still going on. (Photo credit: Pinterest, Philippine paintings, Online.)

Typical Filipino nipa hut in a rural village and carabaos pulling a sled, 1900. (Photo credit: Pinterest, Old Philippines, Online.)

T'boli girl, Mindanao. (Photo credit: Pinterest, online.)

T'boli women musicians. (Photo credit: Pinterest, online.)

 T'boli children. Note the weave of the boy's dress, made from hemp (a banana-like plant with very strong fiber) which are similar to the Manobos of Bukidnon and Mandayas of Davao, Philippines. (Photo credit: Pinterest, online.)

 Tubad, a family ceremony, among the B'laan of Bukidnon, Central Mindanao, Philippines. Note the weave design of the clothes which is similar to the design found in other Austronesian groups in the Pacific and in Southeast Asia. Note also the guitar which also has the same design as in other Austronesian groups. (Photo credit: Pinterest, Philippine Culture, Online.)

Filipina workers stripping tobacco leaves in a Manila factory, 1900. (Photo credit: Pinterest, Old Philippines, Online.)

Part Four. The Philipines Today

Fast forward to 2015:

Pia Alonso Wurtzbach, above, an Austronesian Filipina with mixed European blood, became Miss Universe on Sunday, December 20, 2015. (Photo credit: screenerty.com, Online.)

The following is a list of **Philippines'** official representatives and their placements at the **Big Four** international beauty pageants, considered the most important in the world. The country has won in all four pageants with a total of **fourteen** victories:

- **Three** — Miss Universe crowns (1969 • 1973 • 2015)
- **One** — Miss World crown (2013)
- **Six** — Miss International crowns (1964 • 1970 • 1979 • 2005 • 2013 • 2016)
- **Four** — Miss Earth crowns (2008 • 2014 • 2015 • 2017)

(Data Source - https://en.wikipedia.org/wiki/Philippines_at_major_beauty_pageants)

(Photo from Malacanang Press Office, online.)

President Digong

And in the May elections of 2016, a new Filipino President was chosen among five candidates. President Rodrigo Roa Duterte got 16 million of 34 million registered voters – a clear majority in a direct, popular vote. With that endorsement, the new President started a "drug war", afraid that the Philippines is becoming a "Narc State".Attention has been called to the possible violation of human rights in this drug war.

He also changed foreign policy: from a very close relations with the United States since 1946 when independence was granted by the U.S., to opening relations also with China and Russia. A shift to Federalism to distribute power to the provinces (to be called "states") is in Congress, as well as the amendments to the Constitution in so far as foreign ownership of business is concerned – among other things. Digong, as he is popularly called, has also initiated the biggest infrastructure budget, so far – P3.5 trillion pesos in a "Build! Build! Build" slogan. Early in his term (2017), the Philippine economy has posted a healthy 6 percent growth, and a fastest growth rate in Asia, according to the World Bank.

Building up from previous administrations – mainly for lack of policy initiatives and lack of infrastructure solutions – traffic congestion in Metro Manila, estimated to cost P4.5 billion pesos a day is one of the pressing issues at the moment. EDSA, for instance, is overloaded with 7,000 vehicles per hour vs its designed capacity of 6,000. A traffic study commissioned by a private car-hire company predicts vehicle flow in EDSA to come to a "standstill" in 5 years (it will "crawl" at 10 kms/hr) if no initiatives – whether by reducing vehicles or building new roads/overpasses, and mass transit systems, if done. The Metro Manila subway is already on the planning table, with financing coming from foreign sources.

The country is still poor and underdeveloped, with high unemployment and poor wages, driving skilled and unskilled workers to work abroad as "OFWs" – "Overseas Filipino Workers". This sector, however, has succeeded in remitting back to their families the highest remittance from any foreign exchange source – higher than manufacturing exports. The Philippines exports its labor.

Globally, perhaps due to the mastery of the English language, Filipinos – laborers, domestic help, construction workers, airport/airline skilled technicians, professionals, etc., - are present in almost all countries of the world. In the U.S., the premier destination of Filipino migrants, it is estimated that they comprise 5 percent of the total population.

The most recent newsbreaker is the "Marawi War" where after 5 months of intense battles, the Philippine armed forces and police destroyed the Islamic Group ISIS which aimed to make Marawi City its foothold on a "caliphate". President Digong asked, and was granted, martial law powers up to the end of 2018 in Mindanao to counter this insurgency. The war with the NPA-Communists still goes on. The peace talks having been suspended.

The 6-year term of President Digong ends in 2022.

Social weather surveys, as of January 13, 2018 indicate his continuing popularity: it's still "excellent" at 75 percent. This is based on a non-commissioned survey held December 2017 that sampled 1,200 respondents. It was up from 73 percent of September 2017.

Secrets of Underdevelopment

The Philippines, despite its present economic growth (6 percent) is still poor and underdeveloped. This could be due to the following:

1. The Philippines is an archipelago of over 7,000 islands and is not part of the Asian Mainland. Within the country, transport and communication requires ships, planes, and undersea cables. While bus travel from Manila to Mindanao uses "RO-RO" of ferries that carry vehicles, it's still a very involved travel.
2. Over 300 typhoons visit the Philippines annually. Some of them, like supertyphoon Yolanda in November 2013 devastated millions of properties and houses. Rains and storm surges flooded towns and cities. Strong winds tore up houses. Four years since, rehabilitation of Yolanda-affected areas have not been completed.
3. Foreign direct investment (FDI) is slow to come into the Philippines because of a constitutional provision that businesses should be owned 60-40 in favor of Filipinos. Singapore did away with this when it became independent in the 1950s, and as a result,

foreign investors came and generated full employment. It also helped that Singapore declared a "duty free economic zone".

4. The separation of church and state is already enshrined in the Philippine Constitution (Art. II, Sec. 6), but there is yet no enabling law to put it into operation. Ironically, the Bureau of Internal Revenue issued a tax-ezemptioon on religious organizations and its personnel. Priests do not file income tax returns, despite amassing millions in unaudited weekly church collections. Schools, colleges and universities owned by churches do not pay income tax.

5. The latest tax reform law, called "TRAIN" did not impose high taxes on the rich. Other countries tax the rich as much as 70 percent of net income. The new tax law kept the maximum tax rate at 32-35 percent. Doubling it could have generated much needed revenue for social programs.

6. Science education is present in schools, but it has not gone far enough to be able to set up a "science industry". Philippine education, except for a few "sciene high schools" has not built a strong and deep foundation for scientific education. We even export our scientists to better-paying industries abroad. Some come back when they retire. Very few.

7. Finally, worldwide studies correlate poverty incidence with religiosity. The Philippines is 85 percent Christian and 10 percent Muslim. The last Black Nazarene procession in Quiapo, Manila – held every January 9, drew 3.5 devotees, most of them poor. They did so in the hope of being granted good luck. They do it every year. And remain poor.

The End

Published and printed by
TATAY JOBO ELIZES,
Self-Publisher, under the expressed permission,
approval and authorization of the authors,
EMMANUEL IKAN ASTILLERO & FRIENDS
who own the copyright to this book. The copyright owners can withdraw or rescind this permission at their discretion without any objection from Tatay Jobo Elizes at any time. Printing of this book is using the present day method of Print-On-Demand (POD) system, where prints will never run out of copies, unless the owners decide otherwise. The copyright ownesr are free to republish or reprint with other
publishers and printers anytime.

ISBN – 13: 978 – 1983837074
ISBN – 10: 1983837075

All rights reserved. No part of this book may be reproduced or copied in any form or by any means without written permission from the Owner and present publisher.

Contact: job_elizes@yahoo.com
Website: http:tinyurl.com/mj76ccq

Printed in Germany
by Amazon Distribution
GmbH, Leipzig